PAUL K. CONKIN

Self-Evident Truths

Being a Discourse on the *Origins & Development* of the First Principles of American Government— *Popular Sovereignty, Natural Rights,* and *Balance & Separation of Powers*

INDIANA UNIVERSITY PRESS

Bloomington / London

*Published in Canada by Fitzhenry & Whiteside Limited, Don Mills, Ontario
Manufactured in the United States of America*

Library of Congress Cataloging in Publication Data

Conkin, Paul Keith.
Self-evident truths.

Includes bibliographical references.
1. Political science—History—United States.
2. Natural law. 3. Representative government and
representation—United States—History. 4. Separation of powers—United States—History. I. Title.
JA84.U5C63 320'.0973 73-16525
ISBN 0-253-35150-2

Contents

Preface

As a historian I am often reminded of childhood, when my favorite game was still hide and seek. Not unlike my youthful and usually well-hidden playmates, the most vital and determinate elements of our common heritage keep running off and hiding, either in our moments of inattention or while we look in other directions. And these hidden elements are so elusive, so difficult to find again. But seek them we must, for without them we are lost in the world, incomplete persons without any clear sense of who we really are.

The most hidden past is often also the most obvious, the most commonplace and conventional. It surrounds us. I find that particularly true for the informing ideals that helped shape and vindicate our early American governments. We retain the governments in virtually unchanged form. We even continue to recite the ideals. But familiarity breeds not only contempt but a blindness to detail or nuance, even as recitation converts meaning into ritual. The very phrases that are most familiar—"we the people," "a government of law," "the natural equality of all men," and "life, liberty and the pursuit of happiness"—are often the least clear because of all the present ambiguities of language. I have found that their eighteenth-century meanings, often so different from today's and so well hidden behind the changing fashions of language, are almost unrecoverable.

More so than in any previous country, the new American governments, born out of war and separation from Britain, conformed to certain very traditional canons of normative political theory. This adherence to theory was a result of peculiar circumstances and not of any peculiar bent of Americans for abstraction. Among other things, this backdrop of theory means that one has to attend very carefully to the subtleties of moral philosophy in order fully to understand the acclaimed source, the intended purposes, and the achieved form of early American governments. These three themes—source, ends, form—constitute the three major parts of this book. I believe that an understanding of these "first principles," to borrow a label of our forefathers', is equally necessary for a full appreciation and celebration of our most basic institutions, at least in their original and ideal status, or for a searching criticism or repudiation of them, either in their original purity or in their subsequent debasement.

Normative theory offers only one very idealistic perspective on American governments. As always, ideals in America often differed radically from achievements, and even on occasion served as insincere justifications for deliberate oppression. Also, beliefs about what is right and wrong in government usually serve as retrospective vindications of choice, or at best determine the direction of choice rather than directly stimulate it. To trace the development of these aspects of Western moral theory that pertain to government is not to trace the history of government. But philosophy has at least been interactive with the development of Western governments. It springs as a uniquely human response from the urgency of events, and subsequently becomes one strand in the unfolding of events, some otherwise forced, or quite adventitious, or the clear result of less abstract calculations of interest. If one wants to understand the multiple causes of the American War for Independence, or the varied practical urgencies that clashed and then blended in our early constitutions, then this book is only a preface.

The focus and object of our historical thinking in large part determines the value of such thinking. Reflection on the highest political aspirations of our forebears almost inevitably forces us to consider our own preferences, our own beliefs about the minimal requirements of a good society. That means a critical evaluation of the ends served by our present political institutions. Or, in other words, the utility of a history of moral ideals is itself critical and moral. Not only does it help to reveal the purposes, the conscious and articulate aspirations, that at one time in the past helped shape our collective behavior, but it also becomes a vital resource in the development of our own taste. It stimulates the type of thinking that leads to new and ever more subtle visions of the good life. In the recent past the most celebrated forms of knowledge have been of another type, those which disclose regularities of behavior in physical and social phenomena, and thus the very forms of knowledge that permit reliable prediction of and effective control over events. Without such knowledge we are often helpless, unable to achieve any goals. But at times technique is surely not as important as vision, and scientific explanation, which arms us for successful action, not as vital as historical knowledge, which reveals ourselves as moral agents in a continuum of cultural development, and which suggests to us ever new aspirations.

In government as in private conduct, our eighteenth-century progenitors believed they should heed a body of principles which revealed to men what they *ought* to do, in behalf of either earthly happiness or eternal bliss. I have selected for treatment only those principles that then seemed universally obligatory and quite apparent to men of good will and normal reasoning ability. The founding fathers believed not that all government authority originates in the people (they knew that this was true for very few areas of the world) but that it *should*, and that in cases where it did not the people were in some sense slaves and governments were in some sense their master. They believed that any government *should* serve obvious and minimal moral ends, such as the protection of life, liberty, and property. Finally, with a bit less assurance and clarity, they believed that only a limited government with certain formal qualities, such as a separation and balancing of powers, could reliably serve these ends. Thus, any responsible people *should* frame governments with these formal properties, even though contextual circumstances alone dictated a wide variety of optional features. These optional features, being relative to time and place and sentiment, are not properly a part of normative theory or of first principles.

Much more than I expected when I began work on this book, I found that these eighteenth-century political ideals still have a beguiling personal appeal. At least at the level of political taste I am not as far removed from the founding fathers as I expected. Not that I have discarded any of the profound doubts I have about present governmental policies or about the functioning of traditional institutions. But surely much more than any eighteenth-century American, I do recognize elements of parochial taste in my political preferences. It is difficult for me to believe that any normative theory is universal, that all right-minded people have to agree with it, that it fits all contexts and all societies. Eighteenth-century Americans could still, without a second thought, read their preferences into the universe, and establish their "rational" institutions as models for the whole world. They searched the past for example and rule, but withal were very unhistorical. They still lived in a world designed by one God and in which men everywhere had the same "nature." They did not see their least-questioned assumptions, their most obvious preferences, as products of a cultural heritage, of the always particularistic experiences and conceptualizations of their immediate progenitors in England or in the broader but still parochial Christian West.

The most gifted of the founding fathers were in no sense fools. They recognized the wide variation of environments and cultures and acknowledged the contextual elements that should help determine the forms of government. But undergirding the variety there was still, in their estimate, a universal content, and thus the possibility of a moral and political "science," of true "first principles." They were at the very brink of a new appreciation of cultural heterogeneity, and thus among the last children of an expanding West who could, out of innocence rather than racial or cultural arrogance, still marshal cosmic support for their fondest aspirations. Perhaps like most contemporary Americans, I respond not only to their image of a good life but also to the coherence and logic of their arguments. But I feel moved to insert a peculiarly modern qualifier: *if*. A hypothetical now has to preface all our affirmations. *If* we still want the same goals, still yearn for the same forms of fulfillment as our founding fathers, then we will still respond to their logic and their prescriptions, for in this context both remain internally consistent and very persuasive.

For readers fascinated with the growing diversity of historical specialities, this book may have methodological interest. It exemplifies a special form of intellectual history. I have tried to identify the earliest sources of such key moral and political concepts as popular sovereignty, natural rights, and balanced separation, or concepts close to the "unit ideas" celebrated by Arthur O. Lovejoy. I have traced these concepts to their technical maturity in the thought of theologians and moral philosophers, showed their increasing polemical value in actual political conflict, and finally revealed their formative influence upon American political institutions during the climactic period of the American Revolution. It was then that such concepts finally gained broad public acceptance and became an integral component of political behavior. But as intellectually assimilated, institutionally implemented, and verbally celebrated concepts they were on the verge not only of crushing new philosophical challenges but also of losing their vigor and radical import, of becoming uncriticized commonplaces in a largely verbal orthodoxy.

I have two all-important acknowledgments. I completed this book during the first months of a senior fellowship granted by the National Endowment for the Humanities, supplemented by a grant from the Graduate School of the University of Wisconsin. I am most grateful for the unencumbered time for searching and thinking. Only my students at the University of Wisconsin contributed directly to the content of this book. They were my sounding board, uncomplainingly listening to my earliest, most feeble efforts to straighten out a bundle of complex ideas, and later serving as effective critics.

I want to combine acknowledgment with a form of apology.

Not without trepidation have I trod in the paths of great scholars, feeling very much an interloper. I will never know as much about the American Revolution or about the variety of concrete issues that informed early American politics as my colleague Merrill Jensen. Only now can I begin to appreciate the challenge accepted by a Bernard Bailyn or a Gordon Wood, who have tried to integrate political theory with the day-by-day clash of factions or with the complicated maneuverings that led to new governments. I do not always agree with them. No matter. I entered their domain as a novice, and now leave it as, at best, a hopeful apprentice.

PART ONE

POPULAR SOVEREIGNTY

The Authority for Government

I. *Biography of an Idea*

Futility usually plagues any effort to discover the origin of the commonplace. The paired concepts of popular sovereignty and natural rights are only subtle elaborations of two simple beliefs—that the coercive authority of a legitimate government derives, ultimately, from the voluntary consent of the people of a community, and that such authority exists only so long as it serves its only proper end—their security, welfare, or happiness. This carefully contrived wording suggests endless qualifications and evokes memories of other, more historically pregnant phrases. It should remind Americans of Jefferson's sweeping and eloquent vindication of our separate national existence: governments derive "their just powers from the consent of the governed"; all men "are endowed by their creator with certain unalienable rights; that among these are life, liberty and the pursuit of happiness"; and that governments are instituted "to secure these rights."

Of the two concepts, natural rights is the more complex, had a much more elaborate development in Western moral and legal traditions, and was a decidedly more useful rationalization for

American independence. But popular sovereignty has both a temporal and a logical precedence (the granting of authority precedes its use), and contributed more to the actual forms of American government that were, and still remain, the most distinctive. Because of their mutual dependence (popular sovereignty is almost always a tool for preserving natural rights), the two concepts rarely exist singly. Analytical clarity alone vindicates their separate consideration.

The developed doctrine of popular sovereignty blended two themes, the ancient idea of popular consent as the foundation of government and the more modern and more abstract concept of sovereignty. Not until 1603 did Johannes Althusius complete this blending. By the eighteenth century, almost all English and American political writers gave lip service to some version of popular sovereignty, but rarely did they use it in a careful or very precise way.

It is impossible to locate the person who first gave birth to the belief that a government derives its legitimate power from the people. Later advocates of this belief found precedents in the biblical account of the Hebrews' deciding to have a monarchy instead of simple judges. Late medieval writers, such as Marsilius of Padua, professed to find the position in Aristotle's *Politics*, but it is there more by implication than by explicit argument. Plato suggested a form of contract in his *Laws*, but surely no developed doctrine about the origin of political authority. Both Aristotle and Plato saw government as a natural, ever-present aspect of human society. They focused not upon the origin but upon the best forms of government, and even more upon the proper end of government, an emphasis that very clearly marked the beginnings of natural-law theories. Their emphasis upon form and upon law continued in the Stoics and in Cicero (of the classical political thinkers he had perhaps the most influence on America).

This concern for ends, for moral achievement, did not go unchallenged. In Plato's *Republic* an arrogant Thrasymachus argued that will and sheer power were the source of law and justice, a position that climaxed in Thomas Hobbes. Later, skeptical members of Plato's Academy joined Epicureans in founding law and political order in variable local customs. There is a hint of popular sovereignty in their emphasis upon tradition and the consensual habits of a people. Here, very early, one catches a bit of tension, if not conflict, between popular sovereignty and natural law. To hold government accountable to the contextual and particularistic will of a people may be quite different from holding it responsible to some universal measure of justice and right. At least by many theories of right, the people may consent to immoral and unjust laws. For one who believes in natural law, consent can never be the sole criterion of legitimacy.

Roman jurists first stressed the foundational authority of the people. They argued that Roman law rested on the will and customs of Roman citizens. Even the edicts of the emperor were law, not because he willed them, but because the people chose this mode of legislation. Even when they argued in a theistic context, with all authority attributed to God, the jurists still acknowledged the intermediate role of the people. Often the fiction of popular consent camouflaged the most arbitrary rule. But incorporated into Roman and later canon law, and elaborated in lengthy commentaries, this position became a dominant thread in medieval legal theory.[1]

Early Christians did not speak with one voice on political issues. The political heritage of the New Testament proved as ambiguous as its theological message. The clearest, most influential, and most debated political sermon was in Paul's letter to the Roman church:

> Let every soul be subject unto the higher powers. For there is no power but of God: the powers that be are ordained of God. Whosoever therefore resisteth the power, resisteth the ordinance of God: and they that resist shall receive to themselves damnation. For rulers are not a terror to good works, but to the evil. Wilt thou then not be afraid of the power? do that which is good, and thou shalt have praise of the same: For he is the minister of God to thee for good. But if thou do that which is evil, be afraid; for he beareth not the

sword in vain: for he is the minister of God, a revenger to *execute* wrath upon him that doeth evil.[2]

Paul's celebration of government and of law cohered well with the views of Jewish and Greek scholars, and continued the Old Testament theme of a sacred covenant. It may also have reflected Paul's concern over anarchic tendencies among Roman Christians. But whatever the controlling influences, Paul spoke to Christians with divine authority and they had to accept his admonitions. Orthodox Christians acknowledged God as the source of law and of government, whether God established it as a natural good or as a divine remedy for human pride and rebellion. Those who governed on earth were special servants of God, His very vicars on earth, and deserving of complete respect and obedience. But did God sanction unjust and tyrannical rulers? Could they be His servants in their evil doing? Since God no longer selected kings and emperors, what was the proper mode for establishing them in positions of authority? Was conquest or the sheer exertions of superior power sufficient? Were arbitrary kings a form of merited punishment for sins? Or did Paul's admonition of obedience apply only to duly constituted and just kings, or those who ruled according to law, in behalf of justice and right?

The answers varied. Among the patristic fathers, Gregory and even at times Augustine supported unqualified obedience. Ambrose and Isidore of Seville made obedience dependent upon just rule. By the ninth century, the Age of Charlemagne, Roman and patristic theories merged with Teutonic customs of election and contractual obligation. From the ninth century to the sixteenth, the idea of unqualified obedience was a distinctively minority view among both civilian and canon lawyers, and among the more able theologians and philosophers of the Western Church. Most theorists believed that the people were the intermediaries between God and king, and that governments originated in a compact or covenant. They emphasized that a government had to meet a moral test, had to rule in behalf of justice, before it could be legitimate. Feudal relationships, contractual and rooted in custom, undermined any absolutist theories of the state. After the eleventh century, the great controversy between the Church and more assertive emperors and kings gave defenders of the Church new reasons to stress popular and legal limits on secular power. John of Salisbury even vindicated tyrannicide against a ruler who used the sword against the people, the Church, and the law.[3]

In the thirteenth-century renaissance, theories of popular consent and natural rights were commonplace. Thomas Aquinas revived Aristotle's emphasis upon government as a positive good and worked out a detailed analysis of eternal, divine, natural, and positive law. Largely on natural-law premises, he justified popular resistance to the point of deposition, and even flirted with the idea of justifiable tyrannicide. He preferred a mixed government, and believed that a community of men, out of something approximating a state of nature, first decided on the form of their government and transferred power to it. Largely in behalf of ecclesiastical goals (the battle against papal supremacy), Marsilius of Padua pushed the idea of popular consent almost as far as did any modern writer. William of Occam believed in popular delegation and the right of resistance. On the very eve of the Reformation, a Frenchman, James Almain of Sens, not only stressed the origin of government in compact and a residual power in the people to discipline and remove governments, but also argued that the people do not have a moral right to surrender complete power to any prince. And so it goes. However qualified, the principle of popular consent was the predominant theory of government origins all the way through that vague entity called the Middle Ages.[4]

Despite the variety and richness of medieval political theory, little of it directly influenced Americans. In basic beliefs, if not in details and in rhetoric, all the great libertarian theorists remained at one with their medieval and Christian predecessors. Had Americans been so inclined, they could have found almost as many needed rationalizations for their independence in

Aquinas as in Locke. Only the fashions of language and the barriers of time and religion made a Locke or a Milton much more appealing. Religious affinities and direct lines of influence also made an array of Continental Calvinists much more usable than an impressive group of sixteenth- and seventeenth-century Spanish Jesuits (Molina, Suarez, Mariana) who preached virtually the same messages at the same time.

The Protestant Reformation added the stimulus of bitter religious strife to political speculation. The first effect of the Reformation seemed to be a strong reinforcement of extreme divine-rights theories. The long-range effect was a reinvigoration of libertarian theory. Circumstances largely determined this paradoxical result. There was never a distinctive Protestant political position. After Luther, Catholics and Protestants could always be found on both sides of any major theoretical conflict. The small spiritualist sects (falsely called Anabaptist) adopted chiliastic goals and briefly threatened the established order. The Brethren, or the true Anabaptists, took Paul's admonition to the Romans quite literally. They not only advocated passive obedience to secular authority, but renounced any political role for the Church, retiring to their separated communities to suffer silently untold persecutions.

The center reformers—Zwingli, Luther, and Calvin—all admonished their followers to render complete obedience to existing rulers, who received their power from God and exercised it as His stewards on earth. Even a tyrant could represent divine punishment and had to be suffered. Calvin and Luther took seriously the Pauline injunction, but also wanted to gain the support of ruling princes and overcome the fears of radicalism produced by extreme sectaries. Luther's very opposition to papal claims aligned him with German princes seeking greater autonomy in the Empire. Lutheranism abetted centralized control in the German states, even as it weakened the Empire and challenged the whole medieval idea of a unified political order to parallel a catholic church. Thus Luther eventually had to give his support to German princes in their struggle against the Empire.

His immediate disciple and successor, Melanchthon, moved even closer to the dominant medieval position—he supported princely resistance when the emperor threatened their religious views, and tempered Paul's mandate to obedience by a test of "justice." [5]

Calvin's political views deserve more analysis, if only because his followers exerted by far the greatest influence upon American political thought. A student of law and scholastic philosophy at the University of Paris, Calvin had views on law and government that were very close to those of Aquinas. God ordained government as a human good but He did not prescribe any particular form. That remained a human option. Calvin favored a mixed form, or an aristocratic republic such as he knew in Geneva, based on a communal covenant and carefully circumscribed elections. Even as he preached on Christian obedience, on the sanctity of the existing order, he reminded Christians of their political obligations and told magistrates that their high calling was from God, and that they had an awesome responsibility to govern justly. He wanted good government. But above all he saw the need for government, good or bad. He feared the disorder and anarchy that might result from individual resistance and popular rebellion. Even a bad government was a cross to bear, for it still brought some discipline and punished for some forms of human evil. Calvin, of course, wanted his followers to obey God and the Scriptures even against secular authorities. But they were to disobey immoral commands passively, in prayer and repentance, and flee to more hospitable countries if at all possible.

Calvin made some seemingly minor qualifications to his admonition of obedience. He solaced Christians with the hope that God, as in times past, might raise up special servants to deliver them from tyranny. It was also quite proper for citizens to seek redress for political wrongs through duly constituted subordinate magistrates appointed for their protection. Such tribunes had a Christian duty to oppose a tyrannical prince. In one sense, Calvin merely authorized people fortunate enough to live under some form of mixed government to use one available agency of that government to check another. The Estates General in France provided a check on monarchical prerogative, and thus a protection for the individual. In France he counseled Protestants against resistance to persecution except when championed by local princes. It was also on this ground that he supported the Protestant princes of Germany in their war against the emperor. His immediate successors would turn these minor qualifications into a vindication of virtual revolution.[6]

Unlike a majority of Lutherans, early Calvinists almost everywhere suffered as persecuted or exiled minorities. They fought back, and in the process added polemical verve to abstract doctrines of popular sovereignty and natural rights. During the brief reign of Mary Tudor, extreme English Protestants (precursors of later Puritans) fled to Calvinist refuges in Geneva or Frankfort and from there urged a radical doctrine of resistance upon their English coreligionists. John Knox also suffered as an exile from Scotland who returned home to back Scottish nobles in their deposition of Mary Queen of Scots in the name of popular consent and natural rights. Knox, in what was to become a typical Calvinist argument, alleged that the great men of Scotland represented the people according to ancient customs. As Knox read St. Paul, the Christian had no obligation to obey an unjust monarch, and particularly one who warred against true religion.

In the aftermath of this Scotch revolution, George Buchanan (1506–1582) turned the reformed position into a treatise on political theory and exerted some direct impact on Americans. Like Calvin, Buchanan found the justification for government in man's social nature and in his manifest need for order and objective authority. God wills a commonwealth and sanctions the magisterial role as one of protection and service. Buchanan assumed the original election of kings, and believed the people by covenant prescribed the limits of his authority. The people should also provide a grand council to act with and advise the king. Even the laws of a state largely derive from the people, from their traditions and customs. Buchanan defined a legitimate monarch as little more than a strictly circumscribed executive officer. By this definition, the Scots did right when, acting through their great men, they overthrew a tyrant.[7]

The sixteenth-century French Huguenots, the immediate heirs of Calvin, developed the largest and most influential body of Calvinist libertarian theory. Their early hopes of reforming the whole French church faded before Catholic militancy. Led by a literate, able, and regionally prosperous French middle class, they had to fight for their very survival against religious persecution and what they interpreted as an arbitrary betrayal of faith by a succession of French monarchs. In part, they fought with eloquent polemics, especially in the wake of the cruel repression of St. Bartholomew (1572).

The Huguenots very subtly altered Calvin's political doctrines. In *Du Droit des Magistrats* (1573), Theodore Bèze, Calvin's most influential French successor, expanded the scope of Calvin's restrained idea of magisterial resistance. Bèze emphasized that the Estates General or lower magistrates had a moral duty to resist a prince who commanded against religion. More important, he generalized Calvin's meaning by arguing that there had been such qualified lower magistrates in almost all past empires. In France, he believed that the people had originally established a monarchy by covenant, and entrusted it conditionally with certain powers. When a monarch violated this trust, power reverted to the nation and to the normally inferior magistry.[8]

Francis Hotman, in *Franco-Gallia* (1573), exhausted the historical arguments. Clearly, in a distant past, the French elected their king. The people had accepted the hereditary mode of succession, but used coronation oaths to affirm the popular origin and contractual obligations of the king. Ancient practices also revealed abundant balancing mechanisms; Hotman therefore argued that the National Assembly remained the highest repository of national power, for it represented the sovereign people and was the prime guardian of their liberties.[9]

The most influential Huguenot pamphlet, the anonymous *Vindiciae Contra Tyrannos* (1579), offered the most emphatic de-

fense of popular sovereignty written up to that time. It argued
that a prince was a vassal of God, governing by His suffrance
and by His commands. A legitimate government rests on two
covenants—one between God, the prince, and the people, and
another between the prince and the people, obligating popular
obedience and justice by the king. The people sin against God
when they disobey legitimate laws; the king forfeits his authority when he breaks his trust. Who punishes an arbitrary king?
No less than "the whole body of the people to whom the king
swears and oblidges himself. . . ." [10] God appoints kings, but
the people establish them, "put the sceptre into their hands,"
and with "their suffrages, approves the election." God would
have it this way, "to the end that the Kings should acknowledge,
that after God they hold their power and sovereignty from the
people, and that it might the rather induce them, to apply and
address the utmost of their care and thought for the profit of the
people. . . ." Princes must remember that they are of the
"same mould and condition as others, raised from the earth by
the voice and acclimations, now as it were upon the shoulders of
the people. . . ." [11]

But even the author of *Vindiciae* agreed with Calvin that individuals could not resist a prince. They have to join lesser magistrates or appeal through representative assemblies. The prince is
thus inferior to the community, but always superior to any one
member of it. Magistrates, at all levels, and however they attain
their position, have a moral obligation to resist tyranny. The
people have an avenue of redress so long as only one magistrate,
even in a distant town or province, is willing to lead them in
upholding a solemn covenant. In such courageous leadership
they in reality defend the covenant for the whole community.
But if no one will lead them, the private citizens can only flee or
suffer, for "resting quiet" and "letting blood" is a lesser evil than
anarchy, than the sedition reflected in individual revolt. If the
king suppresses all local magistrates, then the people should
raise up new leaders. If a tyrant invades from outside, then even
private individuals are free to oppose him, for they are not in a

covenanted relationship with him and have not promised obedience. The *Vindiciae* does not anticipate any lack of magisterial
leadership, and allows even a foreign prince to come to the res-
cue of a persecuted people in another country. For "piety commands that the law and the Church of God be maintained. Justice requires that tyrants and destroyers of the Commonwealth
be compelled to reason." Love also dictates "the right of reliev-
ing and restoring the oppressed. Those who make no account of
those things, do as much as in them lie to drive piety, justice,
and charity out of this world . . . ." [12]

One must emphasize that this Huguenot emphasis upon the
power of the people was only contextually, and not inherently,
radical or subversive of the existing order. The covenant concept, in most ordinary situations, heightened a people's sense of
loyalty, sharpened and gave urgent religious content to their
perception of obligation. In fact, the Huguenots affirmed one
type of divine-rights theory: God was the source of authority,
and the sanction of God rested upon the commands of a duly
constituted prince. When people elected magistrates they only
elected to a divine office. It was not the people's power that was
bestowed. A just prince never commanded in their name, but in
the name of God. Rebellion was still a terrible crime and a mor-
tal sin.

Another qualification is in order. The ancient respect for
popular will, whether reflected in custom, in compact, or in
tacit consent, always assumed a community, an organically related body of people, sharing a common body of basic beliefs
and unified by these beliefs despite differences of class and
worldly interests. A common religion, at least so long as men
and women took religion seriously, seemed a minimal cement
for communal order and a minimal basis for any consensual government. The Huguenots never embraced any form of pluralism, any accommodation with wide differences of basic belief.
Their cry of tyranny was lost when the vast majority of French-
men did not feel any such tyranny. But their goals would not be
possible in a heterogeneous society either, one in which there

was no clear public, no covenanted body of people, but only competing interest groups. There was no good answer for minorities such as the Huguenots unless they could create separate, almost autonomous political units. Accommodation within a community for widely different ideologies and interest groups, never easy, would only be possible with religious toleration, political parties, and electoral politics, all of which were as foreboding to the Huguenots as to their royalist opponents.

The double-edged cut of Huguenot theory was clear after one of their own, Henry of Navarre, became king, and by the Edict of Nantes guaranteed a wide degree of autonomy to Protestants. Then, with a favored prince, the Huguenots emphasized his divine calling and the obligations of obedience. In the seventeenth century, as their fortunes declined and renewed persecution took its toll well before Louis XIV repealed the Edict, the Huguenots desperately sought royal favor as their only hope, and took the lead among those who favored royal absolutism. Perhaps conditions and not theories had changed. To balance what seemed a reversal, it was the French Catholics who, after Henry IV took the throne, used popular sovereignty as a weapon against a heretical and thus illegitimate monarch.

Jean Bodin hardly invented the concept of sovereignty, but he was the first person to subject it to careful analysis and make it a central theme in political theory. In his *De Republica* (1576) Bodin defended royal prerogative against the Huguenot "radicals." He reacted against the turbulence in France, and sought order. Already, as revealed by the *Vindiciae*, the Huguenot rebels distinguished sovereignty, or the supreme law-making and king-making power in a state, from the honorific title of "sovereign" which almost everyone still applied to the king. Bodin emphasized this supreme power and the principle of unity that is required. In any commonwealth there must be one supreme authority, with the power to give and enforce laws. This power may rest in one, in a few, or in the many. Bodin did not deny that such power inheres in the community, but he argued that the people may transfer it to one or a few. By the very meaning of sovereignty, its power is indivisible and supreme. There are no mixed governments from the perspective of sovereignty, but only complicated modes of administration. Bodin acknowledged that a sovereign people can use a compact to limit the powers of a prince, but in this case they retain sovereignty rather than divide it.

Bodin's political objective was clear. He believed, unlike Hotman, that the French monarch was sovereign, that the French people had transferred full powers to him, without limit or right of recovery. He admitted that few other countries had such an absolute monarch, that in them other branches of government were not so clearly subordinate and derivative. Bodin honestly believed that an absolute monarch offered the best prospects for social order and happiness, the best cure for civil war and strife. He hoped to use his analysis to cement popular loyalties to the king and mute all notions of dependent delegation and popular recourse.

Bodin did not push his analysis to its logical limits. He located the origin of all positive law in the will of a sovereign, which as creator of such law is necessarily above it. Here, at least, power makes right. He thus challenged the strong medieval tradition that made custom binding over legislative will. But unlike Hobbes, he was unwilling to challenge divine and natural law, or the force of objective right. Even the king is subordinate to God, and under moral obligation to God's commands and the universal rule of right reason. Thus, even an absolute king has no right to be arbitrary. Bodin's mixture of moral and descriptive categories made his analysis confusing. The sovereign, whether a popular majority or a monarch, physically can or cannot obey a higher moral law. Presumably, the "disobedient" sovereign suffers the eventual wrath of God, or flounders in the dire consequences of its "irrationality," but as a matter of power it can do what is morally evil and ultimately foolish, for it alone has the power to carry out its desires and can suffer no limits to its prerogatives. Presumably, the people do not have a moral obligation to obey an evil sovereign, and can feel free to seek means of redress.[13]

Bodin upheld natural law but wanted to undermine traditional theories of popular sovereignty as they operated in France. On this issue his most persuasive protagonist was Johannes Althusius (1557–1638), the Calvinist chief magistrate of the German city of Emden, the Geneva of Germany. Althusius wrote in a moderate, reasoned style. Although influenced by the growing body of Calvinist political literature, including that of the Huguenots, his balance and juristic competence, his academic mien, placed him in the company of a later body of professional jurists such as Grotius, Vattel, Pufendorf, and Burlamaqui. Unfortunately, he bequeathed little of his precise analysis to Americans, who rarely even mentioned his name in their pantheon of political heroes.

Althusius kept the idea of sovereignty and used it as his prime analytical tool. To refute Bodin, he made a careful distinction between sovereignty and the powers of sovereignty. No government is rightfully sovereign, but any government of a commonwealth, by definition, has to have some of the delegated powers of sovereignty. The people, or the whole realm, always *possess* sovereignty, and by right cannot alienate it any more than one can give away his life. This moral emphasis means, practically, that any government that exceeds the powers delegated to it or the ends for which it exists cancels the normal, Christian obligation of obedience, even though as a matter of sheer power (control of an army) it may be able to coerce the people and thus attain its arbitrary ends. The people, he believed, cannot want a tyrant, cannot in good reason bestow absolute and arbitrary power on any government or give up the right of resistance. No single person, no select group, not even a numerical majority can possess sovereignty. Anyone who claims it cannot be a legitimate magistrate, and by such an arrogant claim reverts to the status of a private person and would-be tyrant.[14]

For Althusius, a commonwealth originates in a covenant or

association by which a people pledge to each other their trust, and their determination to attain a harmonious social life, a "life lacking nothing either necessary or useful." Like most Calvinists, he recognized both the necessity and the positive good of government. He knew men needed discipline, or a great deal of governing, and stressed the divine status of human government. As a magistrate himself, he also emphasized the high calling, the awesome responsibility of one who sat in God's place on earth. For "the Commonwealth or realm does not exist for the king, but the king and every other magistrate exist for the realm and polity." [15] God does not stipulate the form of government; the sovereign people choose. And they may choose to assign the powers of sovereignty to more than one government. Part of an elaborate federation himself, he echoed Calvin's republican or presbyterian preference for upward ascending levels of power, and for direct popular participation at the bottom. Since the sovereign people delegate their powers of sovereignty, but retain possession of it, they may distribute portions of this power to different governments without in any sense threatening the unity and indivisibility of sovereignty, a position clarified in America by James Wilson and John C. Calhoun.

Althusius, unlike so many later adherents, never confused popular sovereignty, a fundamental principle of government, with democracy, an optional form of government and one Althusius never desired. But he did realize that popular sovereignty requires more than an original unrecoverable grant of power to a government. There has to be some form of popular recourse whenever a government violates the terms of the grant or violates natural law. In a monarchy he desired a lower order of magistrates, in some way elective or at least representative, to check royal power and provide an outlet for the popular will. No more than the Huguenots would he violate the Calvinist caveat against individual resistance. As Althusius looked at various European governments, he found some aspects of mixed government in them all, for in each there were estates, parliaments, or some formalized lower magistery. Thus, absolute monarchy was not only wrong in principle but nonexistent in fact.[16]

However assiduously Althusius used consent and law to set limits to governmental power, he never wanted any type of direct popular government. The people and their legitimate magistrates, who received talent and calling from God, had a mutual covenant of obedience and justice. So long as the magistrate used only the powers granted to him, and in behalf of moral ends insofar as his abilities permitted, he deserved complete respect from all citizens. In no sense was the test of legitimacy a matter of popularity, of pleasing the people. The whole idea of covenant, of ultimate popular consent, was a tool for cementing such loyalty and sense of obligation that a private citizen would accede to the often grating demands of the social organism and of its "called" leaders. It was a tactic for making men more governable, not more rebellious. If popular opinion determined magisterial judgment, then the people in fact governed and, in the famous plaint of John Cotton, there were none to be governed. Direct democracy, in which popular majorities govern, unchecked by compact, law, or the opinions of the talented, was an excellent example of the absolutism that Althusius abhorred. In such a democracy will and power make right (but, as Althusius insisted, not moral right), just as much as under an absolute monarch. In light of these attitudes, it is no surprise that Althusius never suggested that changes in public taste were sufficient justification for a change in the compact of government. Only when a prince violates the compact or dies do the people normally exercise their sovereignty. Althusius did not conceive of some formal institutionalized mechanism by which the people could routinely make constitutional decisions.

With Althusius, popular sovereignty became a formally complete doctrine, although it suggested many implications that he never explored. For Americans, Althusius is particularly revealing, for his 1603 treatise paralleled the beginning of English settlement in America. His theories about government are almost indistinguishable from those of the Puritan leaders in New England, and reflected the maturity achieved after nearly a century of Calvinist reflection on politics. In one sense he added little to his antagonist, Bodin, except a different order of preferences. Morally, Bodin wanted a complete surrender of sovereignty by a people; Althusius said a moral people could not surrender their sovereignty. For a people in a mind to do so, his admonition has the same force as moral preachments against suicide for one about to leap. His main addition to Bodin was a useful distinction between sovereignty and its powers, and thus his denial of rightful sovereignty to any government. Analytically, Bodin could simply define any government acceptable to Althusius as one in which the people retained sovereignty for the simple reason that they governed. Yet, there is a logic in Althusius' insistence that residual sovereignty in a people is quite distinguishable (and for clarity must be distinguished) from government, the ongoing legislative and executive process.

Althusius' basic principle, that governmental powers originate in the people, remained commonplace in seventeenth- and eighteenth-century England, as basic to a Hobbes as to a Locke. But few were as able, or as willing, as Althusius to combine the idea of consent (essentially a moral concept) with the idea of sovereignty (essentially an analytic and descriptive concept). Hobbes combined them only to prove their essential incompatibility. Even Locke failed to maintain Althusius' distinction between sovereignty and government. He followed the majority of English theorists up through Blackstone into a dead end of parliamentary supremacy, a position that did justice to sovereignty but at the expense of *popular* sovereignty. The English substitute, struggling to the fore even in Locke, would be a form of representative democracy, balanced by that oldest of English antidotes to tyranny—law, both customary and natural.

Richard Hooker (1553–1600), in his multi-volumed, vernacular *Ecclesiastical Policy*, opened a century of English political disputation with a measured, eloquent defense of consentful government committed to natural law and equity. His volumes, in part published after his death, supported both a moderate Anglican settlement and the moderate monarchy of Elizabeth. His views on law were close to those of Aquinas and Calvin. Normally, he saw government originating in consent, either explicit or implicit. The people contract power to those who govern, but the authority itself is from God. Either an express compact or traditional customs limit the prerogative of a ruler, but his greatest obligation is to right or justice. Hooker was the principal medium for transmitting the dominant medieval theories of consent and natural law to Locke and Sidney, both of whom rightfully claimed the weight of tradition for their libertarian doctrines.[17]

The Puritan revolution in England elicited more than its share of polemical political literature. Much of it involved appeals to natural rights or to the sovereignty of the people. James I not only offered a challenging defense of divine absolutism (revolutionary in the English context) but also defended monarchy as a form of government. The more radical supporters of Cromwell, plus such independents as the Levellers, fought for individual rights and worked for political reforms, or for something closer to a representative democracy. But in the final battle with the Stuarts, popular sovereignty had to be the most crucial rationale for deposing and beheading a king. The ablest spokesman for this revolution was John Milton, who simply adapted by then orthodox Calvinist theories to the English context. He used many of the same phrases as the Huguenots. Milton insisted that the king had power from the people, who chose and could depose. The right of reigning was "visible only in the people." He preferred a mixed government, but from bitter experience came to oppose a hereditary monarch as its executive official. Like the Huguenots, he looked to a magisterial class as the support for good government, or to an aristocracy of talent, ability, and righteousness.[18]

In the aftermath of the turbulent and repressive Commonwealth, Restoration England was receptive to theories of divine rights. Robert Filmer, the strawman of Sidney and Locke, wrote his *Patriarcha* before the climax of the English Revolution, but it was published only in 1680. Filmer, like James I, directly challenged any doctrine of popular sovereignty. He denied the origin of government in compact, and denied any right of resistance to individuals or to subsidiary officials, who could only advise the king. But Filmer, like most other defenders of divine rights, did not interpret absolutism as a mandate for arbitrary government. The king had duties and obligations as mandated by God. But only God had the right to enforce His law.[19]

Hobbes rejected any higher law. For this reason he was the most revolutionary theorist of the seventeenth century (Spinoza had come very close to his position). But Hobbes's major heresies involved his conceptions of law and right, rooted in a new theology, and not his ideas on popular sovereignty, which were very close to those of Bodin. Hobbes accepted the original sovereignty of the people and believed actual governments originated either by compact or by conquest. When an insecure and unhappy people, existing without government, without coercive laws, prudently consent to join in political union, they surrender their individual sovereignty to a government, be it an absolute monarch, an aristocratic council, or a popular majority. The newly created sovereign has absolute power, and this power is the source of all law, a necessary precondition for order, peace, and the possibilities of human security and happiness. To Hobbes, the very rhetoric of an ongoing popular sovereignty smacked of nonsense, unless one used misleading language to express a preference for democracy as a form of government. Even in a democracy only an operative majority could be sovereign. A derivative and limited government was not really government at all, but only a tool of those who held supreme power in the society. Judged by private preferences, a citizen may suffer under a sovereign, but that is the necessary price of social order, the hazard of being part of a commonwealth. But such private frustration does not give one any right to resistance so long as one is physically free (not chained, bound, jailed).[20]

The most courageous defender of popular sovereignty

against Filmer, or residual power in the people against Hobbes, was Algernon Sidney. He might be called a martyr to popular sovereignty. He opposed the usurpation of power by Cromwell, and then so untactfully advertised the doctrine under Charles II that he was accused, convicted, and executed under a vague charge of treason. He left a long, often eloquent, discourse in which he adhered much more strictly to the logic of popular sovereignty than the more famous Locke, and in which he considerably expanded the scope of the doctrine.

In most respects Sidney followed Althusius, Hooker, and Milton. He acknowledged both medieval and Calvinist sources for his ideas, and refused to bend before Filmer's contention that discredited Papists and Puritans had cooked up popular sovereignty (Filmer called it "popular sedition"). According to Sidney, God gives power immediately to the people. They select the form of government that seems most likely to procure their happiness and retain a right to judge the performance of that government. "Nations have a right to . . . constitute their own magistrates;" the magistrates then "owe an account of their actions to those by whom, and for whom, they are appointed." [21] Unlike the Huguenots, Sidney did not restrict this recourse to the leadership of lower magistrates, although he seemed to assume that the gentry would act in behalf of the people. Sidney ridiculed Hobbes's idea of irretrievable surrender. God had not created man in such a state of misery that he had only a horrible choice between an empty and insecure natural liberty on one hand and abject slavery and peace on the other. Instead, men twice covenant—once to create an organized society and a form of government, and then again to set terms of obedience and responsibility between the people and the government.[22]

Sidney explored new dimensions in popular sovereignty. Even in Althusius the people had to obey a duly constituted magistrate who governed according to law. Popular sovereignty could only become operative in cases of bad faith, or in fundamental changes inserted at the time of transition between one magistrate or assembly and the next. Sidney asked for some form of constitutional process always open to the people. They can, he said, "meet when and where, and dispose of sovereignty as they will," for the choice of governmental form is always open to them. They may change the form to match changed circumstances, changes of "times and things," or to meet new preferences or tastes. They may even use their sovereignty to restrict elected assemblies, such as Parliament, for all constitutions are open to corruption and will perish without timely renewal and rededication to their first principles. The import of this argument is that a sovereign people, in the midst of a just reign, could abolish monarchy. To deny a "free people" this right is to deny that there is anything of right in any government they establish, an amoral approach to politics deserving only of a Hobbes. Finally, in one tantalizing section, Sidney suggested that the people are the final judges of a magistrate's compliance with the compact or with natural law, but they usually effect this review through courts and juries.[23]

Locke, although an eloquent spokesman for the idea of consent, did not push the idea of popular sovereignty nearly so far as did Sidney. In many respects he adhered to the logic of Hobbes, and revealed more ambivalence on popular sovereignty than he did on natural rights, where he made his most important contribution to modern political theory. Locke, of course, never doubted that ultimate sovereignty resided in the people, available to them whenever their government invaded their natural rights or violated a specific delegation of power. But even here he was far from clear.

When Locke composed his *Two Treatises* (probably just before the Glorious Revolution of 1688), the idea of a compact, usually related to a pregovernmental state of nature, was commonplace. But Locke's predecessors, primarily Calvinists, had used the idea of a covenant or compact in at least three distinguishable ways. First, there was a covenant which established a civil society, a covenant of good faith at least between all contracting individuals (the Huguenots made God a party to it). This originative covenant or social compact might or might not specify the form and responsibilities of government (Sidney seemed to assume that it did). But it was possible and, for reasons that Locke appreciated, convenient to make decisions about the form of government in a second compact. The prime difficulty in combining the two is the unanimity principle that is morally necessary for the social compact (a society has no legitimate claim over an individual unless he explicitly or tacitly consents to be part of it), but almost impossible to attain in decisions about a form of government. Finally, both the Huguenots and Sidney identified a contract between ruler and subject, a covenant of mutual duties and responsibilities.

Locke talked of only one, simple compact. In it, individuals in a state of nature unanimously consent to be part of a unified community, under one government, which thereafter acts in the name of the whole people. Unless the compact stated otherwise, that meant a grant of power to the majority. Locke did not make clear whether this original compact includes, among its terms, the form of government. It seems not, for he had the newly empowered majority enact the "first and fundamental positive law of all commonwealths," the establishment of a legislative power. Locke thus only hinted at a second or governmental contract.[24]

What is clear is that Locke carefully restricted the practical import of popular sovereignty. He emphasized that the legislative power is supreme in a commonwealth. The people surrender to it the right to make all laws, and normally are under complete obligation to obey its handiwork. Locke was almost as concerned as Hobbes to have a government that could really govern, and one that in ordinary circumstance would be beyond any extraordinary control or challenge by the admittedly sovereign people. That does not mean that Locke feared popular participation in government. He preferred a form in which the people elected their legislature. But he wanted them to participate through duly constituted mechanisms, not by adventitious tamperings with the constitution. They could tamper only in dire circumstances—when the government clearly violated natural rights or exceeded delegated powers. The moral limit remained.

What Locke meant, practically, was that individual obligation did not extend to "illegal" acts, and that in these circumstances an individual had a moral right, even a moral duty, to resist or depose a government. He apparently saw no likelihood of such desperate recourse against an elective, representative legislature, and thus viewed popular sovereignty primarily as a residual and extreme protection against princes.

Unlike Sidney, Locke allowed the people no optional recourse to a governmental compact. Only clear usurpation of power vindicates an exercise of power sovereignty. It applies only in revolutionary emergencies. "In all cases," he said, "whilst the Government subsists, the Legislative is the Supreme Power. For what can give Laws to another, must needs be superiour to him. . . ." [25] This position is close to an assertion of governmental sovereignty, and places Locke somewhere before Althusius in the development of consent theories. Locke simply had no conception of constitutional conventions, written compacts of government, or routine processes of amendment and review, all of which Sidney at least suggested.

Two eighteenth-century jurists, Blackstone and Vattel, each exceedingly influential in America, reveal the logical outcome of the divergent emphases of Sidney and Locke. Blackstone could see no legal or constitutional way to limit the sovereign power of government or, in the British context, the power of Parliament (Commons, Lords, and king). If Parliament were the supreme legislative body, then the people could not call it into account. They had to obey it. If they had a right to challenge it, then clearly it was not sovereign and not a competent lawgiver. So far he followed Hobbes. But Blackstone was in a legal tradition that stretched back through Coke to Fortescue to Bracton, a tradition that gave preeminence to law over sheer will. Unlike Hobbes, and in alliance with Locke, Blackstone did find meaning in the idea of "tyranny." The remedy for it was indeed a resumption of sovereignty by the people and a dissolution of an existing government, which, in effect, happened in 1688. But he emphasized that such a resumption, however necessary morally, could not be legal in the normal sense of the word, and no legal system could provide for such an extraordinary expedient. Blackstone, much more than Locke or his medieval predecessors, distinguished "legal" from "moral," and by so doing removed some of the ambiguities usually present in the word *law*. Unlike Hobbes, Blackstone retained the moral. As long as a government continues, until a revolution actually occurs, it can do no legal wrong. Its will is law. A justified revolution is an "extralegal" resumption of power by a suffering people. No more than Locke did Blackstone conceive of separate, ongoing constitutional processes that ruled over normal legislative processes. Power to the people simply meant electoral power, not a "right" of frequent revolutions. Blackstone was as far as anyone from anticipating imminent constitutional developments in America.

In most ways the Swiss jurist Enrich de Vattel understood all the implications of popular sovereignty and was the best recent source of clarity for men like John Adams. Vattel tried in his *Law of Nations* (1758) to perfect a natural system of international law, building upon the work of Hugo Grotius. In an almost incidental preface, he summarized what he believed to be obvious constitutional principles, but ones at almost opposite poles from Blackstone.

Vattel argued that the people of a society, already bonded together by a covenant or social compact, establish the basic order or constitution for their state. They draw upon experience and habits as much as upon theory or deliberation. In ways that please them, they establish the form for, allocate the tasks within, and determine the extent of their government. These formative decisions constitute what Vattel called the "fundamental laws." They share with positive or civil law the element of convention or contextuality, but have much of the sanction and permanence of natural law. Vattel did not mandate a written compact, but in language reminiscent of Jefferson he emphasized that the fundamental law ought to be precise and plain, venerated by everyone in the society with almost religious awe, and jealously guarded against insensible changes and a resultant loss of its original meaning.[26]

In these summary guidelines Vattel distinguished a special constitutional process that supports and regulates normal legislation. In forming their fundamental law, the sovereign people participate in a process much more serious than any election. Vattel, like Sidney, believed that if a nation were unhappy with its fundamental law it could amend it at will, but much more than Sidney he stressed that it should not do so lightly. If a change is unanimous (almost inconceivable), there are no problems. But in almost all cases it has to be a change by a majority or some large preponderance of the whole. Such amendments, touching the basic form of government, should not violate the intentions expressed in the originative covenant (here he meant natural rights or customary ends and purposes, which are a commitment to everyone in a society). Also, after basic changes in the fundamental law, losing minorities should have the right to quit the society and to sell their property and take the proceeds with them. Vattel, in an admonition variously repeated in America during the debate on state constitutions, emphasized that such amendments had to originate in the people and not in a legislative body, which derives all its power from the fundamental law (the only exception would be when a people expressly delegate such power to a parliament). Any prince or assembly that violates the fundamental law loses legitimacy, and places itself in a state of war against the people, just as much as if it had violated natural law.[27]

With Vattel, the concept of popular sovereignty had the full range of meaning that it would shortly possess in America. In summary, the concept entailed the following: (1) Sovereign power rests originally in the whole people of a commonwealth, in a community founded on consent and mutual trust. (2) The people originally exercise their sovereignty by establishing the form and specific powers of their government. This fundamental law must not violate natural law, or the minimal ends of any society, but is superior to all positive or statutory law. (3) Popular sovereignty does not necessitate any particular form of government, and certainly does not require any form of democracy, but it does make any government fiduciary, a limited trust, with effective powers of sovereignty but never itself sovereign. (4) The people have continuous access to the fundamental law, either to change it entirely or to amend it. But, because of the immense significance of such changes, they should not act lightly or without due deliberation.

The next stage of development for the concept was not in the area of theory, but in practical implementation. It was not in Europe, but in America.

2. *In Defense of*

Independence

THE TWIN THEMES OF AUTHORITY and right dominated the war of words that, from 1764 to 1775, preceded the American War for Independence. Always at issue
were resented British colonial policies. The most convenient and
compelling colonial arguments involved equity, fairness, and
justice, and thus the moral quality of British policies. The best
appeals were to avowedly universal standards of right (natural
law) or to ancient and revered British customs and conventions.
Closely related to these appeals were American denials of parliamentary legislative authority over the colonies. These denials involved conceptions of sovereignty and popular consent, if not a
precise idea of popular sovereignty.

Confusion over issues of sovereignty did not mean significant
conflict over the basic principle—government by consent. It is
always perilous to allege a complete consensus on anything, particularly in America. In the eighteenth century there was never
any common ideology, any definable "American mind." To
refer to one is to grossly distort our past. But few articulate
Americans, those with time for reflection and the ability to write
articles or pamphlets, challenged a near truism—government
rests on the consent of a people. Only a rare royalist like Jon-

athan Boucher, an American disciple of Filmer and of patriarchal absolutism, exemplified a truly divergent point of view, and he was an embarrassment for most loyalists.

As one would expect, doctrines of popular sovereignty flourished in Calvinist New England. Either because of direct influences or through deductions from common premises, Separatist and Puritan leaders in New England echoed the political concepts of their immediate predecessors—the Marian exiles, Knox and Buchanan, and the Huguenots—and of the almost contemporary Althusius. They anticipated much in Milton and Sidney. More generally, they were part of Western Christendom, and shared general ideas of consent and natural law, ideas common to many Roman Catholics and to less reformed Anglicans. But the extreme Calvinist emphasis upon calling and covenant gave a distinctive flavor to Puritan political theory. The early leaders, and most clearly John Winthrop, preached what might be called a Calvinist version of divine rights. All magisterial authority comes from God and has to be exercised in His name. The covenanted people establish both the form and powers of government, at least in the few areas beyond God's own revealed law and what is apparent to right reason. Thus, one necessary aspect of government is its limits, its rigidly circumscribed prerogative, and also its nonarbitrary, objective, lawful character. The other aspect is its tremendous power to discipline and order, its quality of great authority within the limits of covenant and law.

At first almost by accident, and then by clear preference, the Puritans in Massachusetts Bay elected all town and provincial officials annually. But, in their theory, this mode of appointment did not diminish the dignity and even sacredness of the magisterial office. One still ruled by authority of God, not popular will, which only determined who would assume this high calling. As both John Cotton and John Winthrop insisted, Massachusetts was not a democracy but a holy commonwealth.

The durability of Puritan political beliefs is astounding. They changed very little from 1630 to 1776, at least among the intellectual elite of ministers. Major schisms in theology had small impact on conceptions of sovereignty and law. Cotton simply opened the long refrain: "All power lies," fundamentally, "in the people." [1] John Davenport, in 1669, located the origin of political power in the people, who measured out only so much as God's word allowed, and who set bounds to its exercise. If government violated the people's conditional trust, they could resume their sovereignty.[2] While Roger Williams diverged on church-state relationships, he agreed on popular consent. He believed government had no more power, and for no longer time, than the covenanting people entrusted to it, for the magistrate is but "the eyes and hands and instrument" of the people, and has not an inch more civil power than that measured out to him.[3] In dozens of election sermons, ministers preached popular sovereignty to both elected politicians and citizens, either to mark the covenanted limits of magisterial power or to stress the respect and obedience due from citizens.

The same theme of consent, and the same moral tenor, the same sense of a holy covenant, continued in the more secular eighteenth century. Rustic John Wise, pouring over a treatise by Pufendorf, stressed that government is the "Effect of Humane Free-Compacts. . . ." [4] In mid-century, Jonathan Mayhew, an Arminian in doctrine, preached a borrowed sermon on resistance that departed not at all from Winthrop's sentiments: "Neither God nor nature" has "given any man a right of dominion over any society, independently of that society's approbation and consent. . . ." [5] In Connecticut, Elisha Williams argued in 1741 that "the Fountain and Original of all civil Power is from the People. . . ." [6] The climax came in January 1776, when the Massachusetts General Court officially denied the authority of the then banished royal government: "It is a maxim that in every government, there must exist, somewhere, a supreme, sovereign, absolute, and uncontrollable power; but this power resides always in the body of the people; and it never was, or can be delegated to one man, or a few; the great Creator has never given to men a right to vest others with authority over them, unlimited either in duration or degree." When kings or ministers or legislators violate the powers entrusted to them by "the original compact . . . they are no longer to be deemed magistrates vested with a sacred character, but become public enemies. . . ." [7]

More significant than the doctrine of consent were new institutions to give it concrete expression. For the Pilgrims, landing in an unexpected part of America, a state of nature became a living reality and not an abstraction of philosophers. As good Calvinists should, they covenanted together in order to have governmental authority in their new village of Plymouth, and in so doing gave enduring fame to the Mayflower Compact. The Puritans at Massachusetts Bay established both towns and congregations by overt pacts or covenants. They brought with them a corporate charter which, by their later interpretation, became a revered compact of government, specifying the categories of magistrates and modes of selection. In 1639 Puritan migrants to Connecticut adopted their Fundamental Orders, an intentional rather than an adventitious compact of government, and at least a good candidate for the first written and popular governmental compact in the modern world.[8]

In Massachusetts, a colony without lawyers and with growing popular resentment of magisterial prerogative, John Cotton in 1636 offered a remedy, a code of laws. But his rejected draft was more than a simple, largely biblical, code, for he also specified the powers and duties of colonial officers and thus tried to amend or qualify the original charter. In 1641 Massachusetts adopted a Body of Liberties composed by Nathaniel Ward, which was a cross between a bill of rights and a code of laws, and thus in no sense a compact of government. But, in a significant precedent, the General Court submitted it to the towns for discussion and amendment, an early form of popular ratification. In 1648 Massachusetts adopted The Laws and Liberties of Massachusetts, which combined the Liberties with a codification of laws already enacted by the General Court.[9] Such written documents did not remain unique. In Pennsylvania William Penn wrote a series of imaginative constitutions for his colony, but unlike the New England documents they were clearly paternal, even feudal, grants and not compacts of a people. The same was true for the abortive frame of government in the Carolinas and for the two British constitutions promulgated by Cromwell.

The revered charters, early neglect by England, a quite divergent ecclesiastical system, and the elective nature of all important officials all reinforced a sense of separation and autonomy in Massachusetts and Connecticut. In 1646 the Massachusetts General Court denied any obligation to the laws of Parliament for those who lived outside England. In 1661 it balanced its avowal of allegiance to a restored Charles II with a claim of legislative atonomy except for laws repugnant to those of England (a vague charter provision). In 1682, when Parliament levied new duties on trade, the House of Deputies (the lower house) passed its own navigation act without mention of Parliament, thus confirming the effect but denying the authority. In 1684 Massachusetts lost its original charter, in part because a special envoy for the king, insulted by his cold reception, found what he believed to be a virtual denial of all British jurisdiction. After the nadir of Governor Andros and seeming threats to almost all their former privileges, all New Englanders joyously greeted William and Mary. But their exact relationship to Parliament remained unclear.[10]

The middle and southern colonies did not have New England's degree of doctrinal uniformity, the continuity of institutions, or the breadth of intellectual leadership. But their colonial leaders had a much closer tie to English intellectual life. Coke, Sidney, Locke, and Blackstone became mentors of a small commercial and planter elite. Here legal theories, as much as theology, shaped political attitudes. Lawyers, not preachers, learned to apply theories of popular sovereignty and natural rights to both internal controversies and imperial conflict. Absent was the special flavor of language so marked in New England—emphasis upon covenant, upon a magisterial calling, upon the sacredness of government.

Popular sovereignty was a common, unifying belief among

diverse colonial leaders. But for those who opposed British policies after 1763, it proved to be an insecure weapon unless they
were willing to claim some type of independence. Almost no
one ever found any way to use the doctrine to support more
generous policies and more local autonomy within a British
commonwealth. Over and over again both sides in the debate
succumbed to an appealing but doctrinally unnecessary dilemma—were the American colonies independent, sovereign
commonwealths, or were they completely subordinate to Parliament as the locus of British sovereignty?

Before untangling some of the doctrinal complexities, one
needs to keep clear the place of moral philosophy in the developing political conflict. It makes little sense to call popular sovereignty or natural rights causes of the conflict. Beliefs about the
rightful source and ends of political authority conditioned the
colonial response to events, provided appealing arguments in the
colonists' effort to gain dedicated adherents to their cause, and
helped shape the new institutions that followed a successful war
for independence. The fundamental principles reveal little about
the motives of the contending parties or, in some present moral
perspective, the merit or guilt on either side. Both the wise and
the foolish, the callous and the magnanimous appealed to the
same principles. The conflict between Britain and the colonies
was not one of principle so much as one of context and fact—did
the policy conflict with the principle? Did British policies really
reflect unprecedented, arbitrary, and thus nonconsentful uses of
authority? Were they basically unfair, and thus contrary to such
minimal ends of legitimate government as life, liberty, and property? Did they threaten a gradual, planned enslavement of
Americans? Were they a natural outcome of English luxury,
corruption, and a waning zeal for liberty? Or, in modern terms,
did British policies amount to a form of colonial exploitation or
economic imperialism? Equally moral men gave contrasting answers to these questions. The Declaration of Independence,
which began with an eloquent statement of moral principles,
ended with a long, highly debatable list of specific British

abuses. Deny the American interpretation of concrete events, and the moral principles remain only as appealing abstractions without revolutionary import.

The developing controversy reached an early climax in the Stamp Act. It symbolized a new British effort to enforce long-standing imperial policy and to raise revenue in the colonies. For Americans, it suggested the ogre of steadily increasing parliamentary control over the colonies, ever less local autonomy, and a great deal less security for such vital interests as property. The Stamp Act also aroused older fears and resentments and embittered contending local factions. Its enforcement provisions threatened an alien, subsidized, and irresponsible bureaucracy. For specific crimes, it threatened the right of jury trial and revived old fears of judicial dependency. The carefully organized and cleverly orchestrated American resistance seemed a direct threat to British authority, an authority reasserted upon the repeal of the act. The issue of authority lingered, through the fight over the Townshend duties, when once again Britain repealed the offending legislation but asserted with even more determination its right to pass such acts. The final climax began with the Tea Act, the Boston Tea Party, and a British response so extreme that it finally seemed to prove the patriot charges of impending slavery and helped unify the colonies for the coming hostilities.

The struggle, polemical and physical, varied in intensity from colony to colony, and took on a special local flavor because of old, internal class and economic differences. Determined conspirators in America used facts and fantasies, in speeches and pamphlets, to inflame the masses. Misinformed British bureaucrats reacted in virtual ignorance, or played into the hands of American insurgents by the very harshness of their retaliation. As always in such conflict, paradoxes abounded. The same Americans who expertly appealed to freedom and liberty often guided mobs in cruel vigilante acts against loyalists, or resorted to intimidation and fear to secure cooperation from the unwilling.

The Stamp Act controversy elicited every theoretical argument used during the next ten years. The mildest colonial objection to the tax, at least beyond practical appeals based on its direct economic effects, denied Parliament's right to impose direct or internal revenue taxes on the colonies. With Daniel Dulaney of Maryland, author of the most influential tract against the Stamp Act, both sides assumed that in England the taxing power was rightly in the House of Commons, in the body that represented those who would pay the taxes. In the well-accepted tradition of Locke, such popular consent to taxes was an analytical implication of the natural right of property. Dulaney, in the language of consent, and by reference to the British constitution, really appealed to natural rights. Taxes constitute a special form of legislation that requires continuing consent. Few Englishmen would have disagreed.

The effect of Dulaney's argument was to shift the issue from authority to right. No legislature has a right to tax without popular consent of some form. British defenders of the tax had to argue, consistent with their own principles, that Parliament did represent the colonists, even though no colonist sat in Parliament because of purely practical difficulties. Parliament represented all Englishmen, including distant colonists as well as numerous home Englishmen who were disfranchised or dreadfully underrepresented. Dulaney accepted the necessity for some forms of vicarious representation. In spite of the close ties of most colonial representation to a geographical area and to demanding, identified constituencies, there were plenty of nonfranchised or underrepresented citizens in America. But in England each class of property holders was represented in Commons. Not so for America. Here the property owners made up a distinct class, a defenseless one so far as taxation by Parliament was concerned. The only practical way that Americans could be taxed with their consent was by their own provincial legislatures.[11]

The distinction between internal and external taxes was disingenuous at best. But Dulaney was not alone in using it. In

London, Benjamin Franklin used it for a clever defense of the colonial position before the House of Commons, as did moderates in the colonies.[12] But the distinction was never important and gained few supporters in America. Loyalists latched onto it, at first to ridicule the distinction, and later to argue that Americans continuously moved from one untenable position to a new and broader one. The next step, obviously, was a denial to Parliament of all internal and external taxing power, again based upon an appeal to natural rights or, what amounted to the same thing, to rights guaranteed in that most nebulous of entities, the British constitution. This argument, which was the more widely accepted one in America, still bypassed the basic issue of sovereignty, but at least did not amount to an open invitation for Britain to increase external duties. It was also an argument the colonists could use consistently to oppose the Townshend Acts.

If the colonies had an official voice on the Stamp Act, it had to be the Stamp Act Congress. It forged a Declaration of Rights and Liberties out of the competing views of emerging radicals and conciliatory moderates. Significantly, it did not distinguish internal and external taxes but simply denied the right of taxation without actual consent. In separate documents the congress acknowledged colonial subordination to Lords and Commons. In 1768, in his famous "Letters," John Dickinson likewise denied to Parliament all taxation rights and made clear that every form of revenue gathering constituted taxation. In his wide-ranging analysis of imperial relationships, Dickinson acknowledged Parliament's power to regulate trade but not to raise revenue, for if American legislatures lost the power of the purse the people would become servile subjects, ripe for revolution. Dickinson's position probably remained the most representative until the Tea Party.[13]

Even as early as 1765 a few men dared challenge all parliamentary legislative authority in the colonies, at least obliquely. James Otis eloquently stated the doctrine of popular sovereignty, but saw no way to utilize it short of revolution and thus conceded Parliament's effective sovereignty. Samuel Adams, later eloquent in his denial of that authority, usually couched his early opposition in the rhetoric of natural rights. Only Richard Bland of Virginia, a reasonable lawyer and professor far removed from the passionate advocacy of Sam Adams, went all the way and claimed sovereignty for the individual colonies, even as he muted the extreme implications of his own position.

Bland started with a state of nature, where all men are equally ungoverned and free. They become subject to government only through consent. One always has a natural right of societal secession, of retiring from an existing state and settling elsewhere in search of happiness. Englishmen, who remained in England and accepted the advantages of that society, gave their tacit consent to the existing constitutional order, one that excluded nine-tenths of adult males from the franchise. But those who left for America moved out from under that compact of government. Nothing in the British constitution, in the ancient laws of the kingdom, or in legal precedents governed mother-colony relationships. The absence of a governing compact meant a constitutional lag at the very least. It also meant that colonists reverted to a state of nature and regained the rights that pertain to it. They were then free to form new states. If they wished, they could (and did) compact a continuing relationship with the English king. The terms of their agreement became their Magna Carta. The colonists came at their own expense and freely formed their own commonwealths, independent in internal legislation but still linked to England by a common "sovereign" and by a unity of external policies. Even parliamentary regulation of external affairs reflected "League and Amity," not sovereign power. The king accepted these terms and gave his approval to internal legislatures with full taxing power. Bland even referred to agreements and charters as the "constitutions" of the colonies. Beginning with the navigation acts, Parliament infringed these rights and tried to make the colonists second-class citizens. But it did so as an act of sheer power, not of right. Paraphrasing Locke, Bland concluded that Parliament, by invading American property, had placed itself "into a state of war" with the colonies. In weakness they might have to submit, but power never made a right.[14]

This claim of colonial autonomy was familiar in New England. John Adams event hinted at it in his first political effort, "A Dissertation on the Canon and Feudal Law." But the first person to argue in the tenor of Bland was an otherwise obscure citizen of Philadelphia, William Hicks. In 1768 he stressed that the power of Parliament rested on the consent of the British people, and that it governed legitimately because of their continuing consent. Americans were not participants in that consent, and thus were under no obligation to obey Parliament. Distance did not abrogate principles; it only required a distinctive American response. If Americans were to enjoy the same rights as Englishmen they also had to have their own consenting legislatures, reflecting the will of the various estates. Since Americans still acknowledged the same king, the result was several countries united in one kingdom. In Hicks, as so often in his successors in Pennsylvania, the doctrine of popular sovereignty almost dissolved into a preference for representative democracy, with the key emphasis upon ongoing consent and even direct representation and not upon popular determination of governmental forms.[15]

Not only Bland but almost every colonial advocate appealed to earlier charters. At the very opening of the Stamp Act controversy in 1764, Governor Stephen Hopkins of Rhode Island (an elected governor) appealed to the terms of his own generous charter, which promised Rhode Island all the rights and guarantees of the British constitution. He interpreted that to mean internal taxing authority. He could find nothing in the British constitution that gave Parliament the right to tax unrepresented Americans or exercise unlimited sovereignty over them. He was not explicit on the scope of colonial autonomy and granted Parliament's right to regulate trade. Unlike Bland, he did not clearly defend the charter as an originative compact of government, but only as a gift of relative autonomy necessary for colonists to retain the rights they had enjoyed in England.[16] The distinction revealed the twofold implication of appeals to charters. If one, with Bland, viewed the charter as an originative compact, then an appeal to it was a concealed claim of local sovereignty and independence, or as radical a claim as one could make. But if one considered the charter as a legal grant made by a sovereign, then one recognized the subordinate status of the colonies. The appeal to charter rights was then only an appeal to consistency, to the sway of long precedent, to the benevolence and moral goodness of a sovereign, but was not a challenge at the level of power. What a sovereign grants a sovereign may take away.

Both Hicks and Hopkins hinted at either a dominion of sovereign states or a British federation in which different assemblies shared legislative powers. A league of sovereign states at least made sense to Englishmen, but as a concealed bid for independence it was totally unacceptable. A federation might have found more favor, but such an arrangement was conceptually incomprehensible not only for most theorists in England but also for most in America. Divided legislative powers remained logically baffling all the way through the Federal Convention of 1787, primarily because of a stubborn blindness about popular sovereignty.

For one versed in Continental theories of sovereignty, even as early as Althusius, the existence of multiple legislatures offered no practical or theoretical difficulties, and in many practical political circumstances were almost necessities. Too often English theorists created a false dilemma by trying to determine superiority and inferiority, when in fact legislatures may be coordinate. A sovereign people may delegate specific legislative powers to a number of different legislatures. The British people (which would include the Americans as a part of the whole) were free to establish any constitutional arrangements they wished. By some form of clear compact, they could have delegated full legislative powers for the English homeland to the existing British Parliament, and simultaneously have delegated internal legislative functions to colonial assemblies. Each legislature would have been supreme within its delegated sphere; neither would have had any authority to usurp the powers of the other. Sovereignty would have remained one and indivisible—in the whole people, where it rightly belonged.

From this perspective Bland was correct. While almost everyone else talked, all too vaguely, of a British constitution, Bland emphasized the constitutional lag. The form of the British government developed either before, or in virtual isolation from, the problem of distant provinces and of provincials who proudly claimed all the rights and privileges of home Englishmen. There simply was no consensual agreement on new institutions that could secure these rights. Americans, as much as Englishmen, were proud of the British system. They believed it was the best in the world. But it had no special arrangements to meet their peculiar needs. Nothing in the long process by which England subjected its king to law and to Parliament added any protection for the colonies.

The problem reflected more than a lag. It also involved an ideological impasse. As emphasized earlier, from Locke to Blackstone most British theorists (and even up through 1787 a majority of Americans also) believed that a supreme legislative power was the very foundation of a commonwealth. In any state or empire all except one legislature had to be dependent and subordinate. This identification of sovereignty with government, and particularly with legislatures, conditioned and confused almost all the controversies between England and America. Americans frequently contradicted themselves, arguing at one moment that the people were sovereign and subsequently assigning the same quality to a legislature. The confusion led practical Americans into conceptual absurdities, such as that reflected in a hundred years of foolish drivel about "divided sovereignty." It led James Otis to an abject acknowledgment of the unlimited power of Parliament only a few paragraphs after he eloquently affirmed the sovereignty of the people. Trapped by this peculiar subjection to an unquestioned doctrine, he had no recourse save violent revolution or pathetic efforts to get Parliament to see its own sins and rectify them. Finally, it led the more daring Americans to what Otis could not yet contemplate—claims of sovereignty for colonial legislatures, a position quite adequate to support independence but one still full of torments when it came time to form a federal union. For the British, the idea of legislative sovereignty led to a fatal black-and-white conception of colonial relationships. Unless the colonists recognized Parliament as supreme in all areas, they necessarily flirted with insubordination and treason.

After the Tea Party and the Intolerable Acts, Bland's position had its years of ascendancy. Blocked by theoretical confusions from any effective appeal for limited but coordinate legislative powers, of even quite restricted forms of home rule, and still reluctant to make a complete break from England, the beleaguered colonists had to claim not only *coordinate* but also *sovereign* legislative powers. The ante was high. Only fervently expressed loyalty to the king left any cement for an empire. Alternatives were few and had only limited support. Much too late in the developing conflict, Joseph Galloway of Pennsylvania, a moderate, sought a plan of union with two coordinate but jointly sovereign legislative bodies, one in England and one in America. But by then (1775) the more fervent colonists wanted more than that, or more than some practical arrangement by which American representatives could sit in Parliament.

Legislative autonomy was the prime demand of the First Continental Congress. Even before it assembled, Pennsylvania, Massachusetts, and Virginia instructed their delegates to press for autonomy and to deny any parliamentary right to legislate for the colonies. This action, in itself, meant revolution. In an early resolution, and in a Declaration of Rights, the congress essentially complied with this demand, although it did acknowledge, as a matter of necessity and colonial consent, continued parliamentary supervision of commerce. By this stand, the congress not only defined as invalid the hated Intolerable Acts, but every act of Parliament touching on the internal affairs of the colonies going back to navigation acts under Cromwell. The severity of the Intolerable Acts and the great sympathy for Massachusetts made plausible the contention that parliamentary legislative power, inflicted as if by an outside agent on helpless people, meant perpetual slavery.

The two ablest and most influential defenders of colonial autonomy were the eloquent and cool Thomas Jefferson and the brilliant and passionate John Adams. Jefferson in 1774 both acknowledged and expanded Bland's 1765 argument. The first Americans took advantage of a natural right of emigration, by choice settled a new country, and there, in a state of nature, established a new society and chose institutions to promote their happiness. They settled America at their own expense, shed their own blood, and gained land and possessions by their own labor. They gained their rights from nature, not from any bequest or grant. Later English aid and assistance, as in the wars with France, were that of any ally, given in behalf of trade and other expected benefits. Such aid gave Britain no title to America. Neither did the fact that the new Americans chose to adopt the legal institutions of the mother country and elected to have the English king as their own monarch. All parliamentary legislation represented usurpation and a form of tyranny. Jefferson indulged a common historical fable—that of Saxon England. Even as the ancient Saxons, Americans came into a new land, there to exercise their right to establish a government of choice and to gain access to an unencumbered, prefeudal form of property. Just as the Normans used force to impose a feudal dependency upon free Saxons, so now Britain was slowly reducing Americans to a state of dependency or slavery. Unlike many colonial polemicists, Jefferson did not exempt the king from all responsibility for America's plight, and in an extended list of specific grievances anticipated both his 1775 Declaration of Causes and the Declaration of Independence.[17]

John Adams, as "Novanglus" in a long newspaper debate with a persuasive loyalist, "Massachusettensis," retraced Jefferson's arguments but added new legal twists. He believed his Pu-

ritan progenitors came into the wilds, resorted to a state of nature, bought land from the Indians, and by their originative
charter established a new government according to their desires.
By choice, they rendered homage to the English king, but in no
sense was Massachusetts ever annexed to the English realm.
Not only was Parliament legally and morally without legislative
power in America, but Americans had never generally acknowledged such authority. For this rather preposterous claim ("Massachusettensis" unmercifully ridiculed it) Adams could at least
cite a few century-old Massachusetts claims of autonomy. Even
parliamentary regulation of trade was on the order of a treaty
between equals. Adams wanted to forestall any loyalist recourse
to the Lockean idea of tacit consent. For Adams, any American
submission to a parliament 3,000 miles away meant an abject
form of slavery. A free man is one bound "by no law to which
he has not consented." Beyond the always baleful subjection,
there was little chance of wisdom or benevolence from Parliament. Adams reflected a type of political jeremiad endlessly
preached in New England pulpits. England was corrupt, lost in
venality and effeminacy. Debts, extravagance, electoral corruption, all testified to the moral decadence of England, and revealed the absence of an earlier vigilance in behalf of liberty. If
Americans acquiesced in dependency, Britain would be the
worst of masters.

Adams also used historical and legal arguments never
broached by Jefferson. He found no basis for British claims that
the colonies were part of a unified dominion or realm. The first
colonies predated the union with Scotland and any British empire or realm distinct from England itself. Americans were not
consulted about the formation of such an "empire," and never
gave their consent to it. From the beginning they gave their
allegiance only to the person of the king, not to any "realm" of
Great Britain. Even the allegiance to the king, expressed in their
charter, was contractual, contingent upon their continued right
to have their own laws and institutions. At the time of the
Glorious Revolution, Massachusetts had her own local revolu-

tion, gave allegiance to the persons of William and Mary, and received a new charter reasserting their rights. They never subordinated themselves to the "realm" or to the British Parliament as the supreme legislator of the "realm." Parliament made William and Mary the monarchs of England but not of Massachusetts. Not that Adams meant to deprecate the effects of the Glorious Revolution; he only emphasized that the people of Massachusetts achieved as much or more by their own exertions and in their own charters. As he contemplated the beloved first charter of the Bay Colony, Adams could believe that Americans had moved beyond the Glorious Revolution two generations before it occurred, and that the principles of the British constitution, falling into decay in England, were to reach their full perfection in America.[18]

Even before he wrote "Novanglus," Adams tutored the Massachusetts House of Deputies in its long debates with Governor Thomas Hutchinson, Adams' most able and most hated political opponent. The issue was sovereignty. Among their arguments, the deputies asserted that the American wilderness was originally a feudal fief of the English monarch, held by him personally and at his absolute disposal. It was not a part of the English nation or realm. Thus, the king alienated it by his choice and with such conditions as he might choose. In return for homage, he granted liberal charters to the Bay Company, charters which allowed complete legislative autonomy. Hutchinson ridiculed this recourse to feudal law as an attempt to reverse two hundred years of British history. The king never held America as a feudal lord but as head of the English state. With advice from Lords and Commons, he was the supreme legislator for the realm, and in this capacity commanded the allegiance of those colonists who came to America and continued to claim English citizenship. These colonists became even more secure in their liberties because of the growth of parliamentary power at the expense of royal prerogative. Surely the colonists did not want to replace a rule of law by an atavistic return to feudal absolutism.[19]

The House of Deputies denied any retreat to a hated feudalism. They referred to a feudal conception of monarchy only because it fit the time and condition of their original migration and helped clarify constitutional issues. They affirmed and embraced the constitutional changes in England up through 1689. Their prime recourse from a seeming return to royal absolutism was their magical charters. Viewed from the perspective of Charles I in 1629, they undoubtedly received their lands as a feudal fief and remained under the absolute will of the king who happily granted them a liberal charter. New Englanders had their own, quite different, perspective. By it, they reverted to a state of nature, purchased estates by blood and labor, and established their government by a free compact. In their charter they accepted the benevolent terms offered by the king and thus consented to a continued, admittedly feudal, homage to him. In a sense they continued this feudal anachronism when they again covenanted with William and Mary. But that covenant meant no substitution of royal prerogative for parliamentary supremacy. They were not royalists in this sense. Even as they debated, Puritan ministers continued to preach against arbitrary princes and to praise the Glorious Revolution as the foundation of their liberties. Should their monarch ever retract charter privileges or threaten their legislative autonomy, the sovereign people of Massachusetts would recompact and sever all ties with the king. That they would do in 1776, when their king refused their petitions and failed to check parliamentary usurpation.[20]

Did these arguments have merit? It is not possible to give any clear verdict. Again, the lack of any identifiable constitutional process in England and the absence of a written compact made all "constitutional" arguments slippery at best. Even the word *constitution* was as full of ambiguities then as it is today. Americans used it in different senses. Charter-conscious New Englanders occasionally used it to refer to a rather hazy compact of government in England. Only the decisions of the Convention Parliament of 1688–89, which added dramatic new restrictions on monarchical prerogative, clearly illustrated a compacting process. New Englanders stressed that they did not participate in that constituent action. And if Parliament was the constituent as well as the legislative body in England, then a lack of representation had a twofold significance. It not only denied colonial participation in lawmaking but also effectively shut the colonists off from any avenues of constitutional redress. They could not initiate amendments or work for basic changes in the system. Other Americans used the word *constitution* for fundamental natural rights and for reserved rights of citizens that they believed a birthright of Englishmen. If written, this form of constitution referred to bills of rights, not compacts of government. Finally, almost everyone at times used *constitution* to designate the form, the underlying structure, of the whole British governmental system, and thus included ideas of balance and separation as well as the whole common-law tradition.

Faced with these semantic difficulties, lawyers such as Adams built their strongest case around legal precedents and historical parallels, particularly in Scotland, Ireland, and the Channel Islands. Local and autonomous legislatures did exist in the Islands, which had retained something close to a feudal dependency on England. Parliament did legislate for Ireland, but colonial lawyers identified a clear act of consent by Ireland, or what did not clearly exist for America. The Massachusetts Deputies also cited Grotius and Pufendorf as juristic authorities; both denied a natural right of legislation to a metropolitan government unless colonies or provinces gave their consent. One eminent constitutional historian, Charles H. McIlwain, believed that the colonists had the stronger case in these arguments, since there existed precedents for their claim and since no clear act of consent existed.[21]

For loyalists, the strongest counterargument involved tacit consent. The colonies had long acquiesced to parliamentary legislation and had not repudiated clear assertions of this right by Parliament. In the Commonwealth Act of 1649, Cromwell's new government made all dominions and territories of the former monarch a part of the realm, and brought all of them under the power of Parliament. Parliament reasserted these prerogatives at the Restoration, and by a Declaratory Act in 1719 extended its sovereignty to Ireland. It exercised these powers not only in navigation acts but also in a series of legislative enactments that either included or singled out the colonies. One could retort, with Jefferson and others, that acquiescence in tyranny by untutored colonists did not make it right. And one could agree with Alexander Hamilton: the very process by which the English people gained power over the royal prerogative helped centralize the realm and lessened the possibilities of autonomy in outlying provinces. But the fact remained that only after 1763 did the colonists mightily protest, and at the very time they least needed the aid and support of the mother country. However meritorious as moral claims, many colonial arguments were incredible as historical assertions. Adams' contention that Americans never acknowledged parliamentary authority was belied by no less than the Stamp Act Congress.

The final colonial refuge in monarchy against Parliament makes up a strange interlude in our history. The numerous petitions to the king surely reflected, not realistic hopes of redress, but the great emotional trauma involved in making a final and complete separation. They did not reveal any new-found love for monarchy or any personal affection for George III. He was at one with Parliament on the question of authority, and was not about to champion the colonial cause. And few of the best friends of the colonies in England, those who had continued to enunciate the same moral principles and who had supported the colonies on specific issues such as taxes, were willing to join them on the issue of sovereignty. They might counsel benevolence, might offer immense quantities of forgiveness, but they did not want separation and could not deny the ultimate authority of Parliament.

By 1774 there was not the slightest prospect of either branch of the British government bending to the American position. More vocal colonial partisans did not want reconciliation, and built an effective insurgency on the strength of British reactions.

They wanted nothing less than effective independence, with or without some nominal relationship with the king. Britain had emotional and economic investments in her colonies. They were part of Britain, and except for a few agitators and conspirators, had every reason to be a happy part. The very logic of sovereignty required the Americans to accept a type of dependency, but it did not preclude wide areas of local autonomy and did not preclude many manifest benefits from the continuing ties to England. Besides, English colonial officials received a very different view of events in America than that presented by a Samuel Adams. They heard endlessly of good and loyal British citizens suffering all the torments of a carefully organized and cynical insurgency movement. They heard of undisciplined mobs, burnings, destruction of property and homes, and deprivation of every form of expressive freedom. The more abstract fantasies of colonial agitators paled into insignificance beside actual, documented examples of majoritarian tyranny. From this perspective, the crying need was local law and order in behalf of protected rights.

The decision for independence removed all the ambiguities. For American patriots the king could now take his place as the hated head of the British nation. He no longer stood as an inadequate symbol for a noble heritage, as the final testimony of the yearnings of a people for the very past they were repudiating. In the Declaration, Jefferson identified Americans as "one people." By the logic of popular sovereignty, all else followed. A people are by right sovereign.

3. Government of the People

Even before hostilities with England became a war for independence, Americans faced the challenges and dilemmas of forming new governments. A decade of political controversy had so agitated fundamental principles of government, had so intensified a commitment to natural rights and popular sovereignty, that Americans were a bit on the spot. They had to live up to all the demands of their professed ideals, ideals that were not always clear in their practical implications. More perilous, they had few precedents to follow.

The withdrawal or banishment of British authority, usually in the form of fleeing governors and councils, left colonies with no duly constituted government. In most colonies only a royal governor could convene a legislative assembly. Thus, in over half the colonies, remnants of former legal assemblies assumed interim power without any clear authority to do so. By the terms of their own theory, the lapse of governmental authority either plunged them into a state of nature or, more consistent with their earlier arguments, left them as covenanted communities without governmental compacts. If still under a social compact, they at least did not have to follow any unanimity principle in establishing new governments. Such niceties of theory had little early importance in many colonies. Not in Massachusetts. There a few people in the western counties did claim the state of nature, and some even found it a delightful state, particularly if they were debtors or faced some discipline under the law.

In forming their new governments, certain guidelines were obvious to all the colonies. Theory as well as the proven utility of written charters dictated a written compact. Also clear in theory was the requirement that any compact somehow rest upon the will of the people. This idea of consent, affirmed by practice or by statement in every new charter of government, gained concrete meaning only through time. Historically, the most fervent advocates of popular sovereignty had not related consent to popular elections or to any type of voting. The Huguenots, for example, assumed a cohesive social order in which the popular will found adequate expression in an accomplished aristocracy, in men of magisterial calling. In the only clear English precedent for overt compacting, the Convention Parliament, the Lords and Commoners had acted for all Englishmen without specific authority to do so and with a sense of the nonlegal and inferior nature of their assembly. Many assemblies in America felt the same insecurity.

As early as 1768 in Boston, and almost universally by 1775, Americans gathered in informal conventions or assemblies, usually to seek redress of grievances or to petition governor or king. These assemblies lacked any authority to legislate or to appoint administrative and judicial officials, let alone the authority to draft constitutions. But now they had to assume the tasks of government or face anarchy. Their only appeal was to the Continental Congress, which also existed in a constitutional limbo, and only gained legitimacy with state ratification of the Articles of Confederation. But in 1775 it was the most authoritative government available. Most of the colonial governments turned to it not only for advice but also for some assurance of their own legitimacy.[1]

In response to requests for advice, the Continental Congress as early as October 1775 suggested that South Carolina call a full and free representation of the people. If they felt it necessary, the colony was then to establish a form of government that would best produce public happiness and most effectively secure peace and good order until the end of the dispute with Britain. The Continental Congress gave similar advice to other colonies in 1775. Finally, in May 1776, in the midst of war and with no early chance of reconciliation with England, it recommended that all colonies without a sufficient government should form one that, in the opinion of the people, would best secure their happiness and safety. It expected some form of representative assembly to draft a constitution but made no distinction between existing legislative assemblies and special constitutional conventions.

Three colonial governments—in Connecticut, Rhode Island, and Pennsylvania—believed they met the "sufficient" criterion. Only two made good on the claim. Rhode Island and Connecticut kept their old charters, which they had long claimed as valid compacts of sovereign communities and which provided for elective governors. With no British officials to expel, and annual elections, they could claim complete continuity in their government. The Connecticut Legislature did celebrate independence by enacting a brief bill of rights. In 1818 the people of Connecticut barely ratified a new constitution drafted by a convention. Rhode Island did not replace its increasingly anachronistic 1663 charter until 1842, and then only as a result of a minor rebellion. The Pennsylvania Assembly, long proud of its near legislative sovereignty, remained in power and claimed sufficiency under the proprietary charter. But the Assembly faced an early revolt, which in effect overturned it in behalf of new constitutional processes.

From 1776 to 1800, fourteen American states (Vermont, Kentucky, and Tennessee included) drafted approximately twenty-five constitutions. The combined states also drafted the federal constitution. Out of this unprecedented frenzy of compacting came a well-nigh ritualized constitutional process, loyally followed all the way to the present. This process, the flesh and blood of popular sovereignty, remains as the most distinctive innovation by American governments. The process includes special, popularly authorized drafting conventions, some form of popular ratification, and either easily accessible amending procedures or convenient ways of reconvening conventions. These constitutional procedures create a special category of law and require a special role for the courts. The doctrine of popular sovereignty, taken seriously, mandated institutions of this general type, but obviously not the exact, ritualistic forms that Americans developed out of a vacuum of political power and the strains and stresses of political conflict.

As the preceding chapters indicate, few Americans ever rigorously analyzed the concept of popular sovereignty or perceived all its implications. No American before Calhoun contributed significantly to the doctrine. But as always, doctrines take on a special clarity as weapons in a conflict. By 1774 the idea of popular sovereignty helped Americans perceive their original charters as compacts of government. As newly independent states formed governments, the doctrine always received lip service, but in states without internal conflict and effective claims by minority factions the ruling elites rarely followed the full logic of popular sovereignty. In all probability, they never perceived that logic. They were able to retain governmental power, draft constitutions either without specific popular authority or without popular ratification, and in most cases use the constitution to legitimatize their continued power. Only the losing and disgraced loyalists vainly protested that they were part of that always nebulous entity—the people.

Pennsylvania and Massachusetts, the two states with the most intense controversy over the procedure for drafting a constitution and over the resultant product, did more than all the others combined to implement popular sovereignty and to make it much more than a pious deference to the power of the people. In these two states vengeful factions sought intellectual and moral ammunition, found it in the sovereignty of the people, and in polemical controversy forced others to perceive the fundamental issues at stake. Given the almost unanimous acceptance of popular sovereignty at the level of abstract principle, the factions that adhered to its obvious, deductive implications usually won the controversies, at first at the level of belief and ultimately at the level of practice. But the only way to trace popular sovereignty to full institutional maturity in the Massachusetts constitution of 1780 is to seek out the earlier, incremental accretions in the various states.

New Hampshire adopted the first constitution. In compliance with recommendations from the Continental Congress, in 1775 the towns of New Hampshire elected a special congress to serve as a temporary government as well as to establish a new form of government. Since reconciliation with Britain still seemed likely, the congress framed a brief, interim constitution in January 1776. Only the popular authorization revealed any zealous concern for popular sovereignty. The same congress that enacted the constitution (there was no ratification procedure) became the legal Assembly by its terms. It, in effect, legitimatized itself.[2] Influenced by Massachusetts, New Hampshire quickly rectified the theoretical deficiencies of 1776. In 1778 a convention drafted a new compact, and submitted it to the towns for approval. They rejected it in 1779 (exactly paralleling proceedings in Massachusetts). The towns authorized a second convention in 1781, and then spent three years discussing, amending, and finally ratifying the constitution. Only the late date—1784—made their procedure less significant than that in Massachusetts in 1780.

South Carolina was next and, of all the states, adhered least to the mandate of popular sovereignty (ironic in light of Calhoun's later insistence upon meticulous adherence in the Nullification controversy). The Provincial Congress, without popular authorization but on recommendation of the Continental Congress, simply enacted a constitution in March 1776 which in effect continued the Provincial Congress in power under a new name and allowed it to choose a legislative council and a president (governor). The contradictions did not go unnoticed. The congress revealed its own doubts. It claimed authority as "a full and free representative of the people," but only barely mustered a majority for this controverted passage. Critics both within the congress and without insisted that a legislative body, the creature of a compact, could not create that compact. The aftermath was a remarkable constitutional interlude. Since the constitution was a legislative act, the new Assembly could amend or revoke it at will. In 1777 it enacted a new constitution. President John Rutledge exercised his power of absolute veto, justifying it on the grounds that the legislature had no authority to enact constitutions. This constitution was the only one in American history to succumb to executive veto. Rutledge resigned with the veto. The Assembly elected a more compliant president, successfully reenacted a constitution in 1778, and in it deleted the executive veto. Only in 1790 did South Carolina elect delegates to a "proper" convention, and finally attain a "real" constitution.[3]

Virginia drafted the first meticulous and enduring constitution. But the people neither authorized nor ratified it, leaving a question as to its legitimacy. Jefferson perceived the procedural flaws and apologized for them in his *Notes on Virginia*. Forty-five members of the former House of Burgesses met in Williamsburg in May 1776 to form a new state government. They worked for two months on two documents, a Declaration of Rights (the most influential ever drafted in America) and a governmental compact. The separation was theoretically proper, for the Declaration affirmed either unamendable universal rights or general principles of government that were not binding but admonitory. The compact, which the drafters with rare precision called a constitution, established the branches and powers of government, which are necessarily contextual and amendable. Yet, the document contained no amendment provisions. Later critics of the constitution insisted that it did not even fulfill the second of the listed rights in the Declaration: "All power is vested in, and consequently derived from, the people. . . ." Only in 1830, after long efforts, did Virginia fulfill this principle by electing a convention to draft a new constitution.[4]

Virginia was the last state to draft a constitution without some specific authority from the people. A New Jersey convention, elected to frame a constitution as well as carry on the normal processes of government, finished its work on July 3, too late to incorporate the language of independence. In 1777 the state legislature amended the document, substituting where appropriate the word "state" for "colony." The change was inconsequential, but such legislative amendment revealed an as yet incomplete separation of legislative and constitutional processes.

Delaware and Pennsylvania made the first dramatic progress toward realized popular sovereignty. Pennsylvania began its convention first (July 15 to August 27, 1776), very much influenced its small daughter state, but took longer to complete its work. In Delaware enough factions distrusted the existing assembly to secure a specially elected constitutional convention (not a precedent, for Pennsylvania had acted first), and then, suspicious of the Tory proclivities of a majority of the delegates, they insisted that the convention limit its activities to the making of a declaration of rights and a constitution (a precedent, since the Pennsylvania convention assumed some governmental functions). In a guarded way, Delaware also initiated amendment procedures. By the terms of the final charter, five-sevenths of the lower house and seven-ninths of the upper could alter the compact. This legislative procedure, of course, bypassed the people, but made clear the superiority of constitutional law over ordinary statutes.[5]

Pennsylvania had the most bizarre constitutional history of all the original states. Untypically, few of the established colonial leaders, many of whom opposed independence, had a hand in drafting the original state constitution. The old, charter-authorized Assembly never willingly relinquished power, but by 1776 saw it erode away as a result of effective challenges by radicals. After 1775 provisional committees provided the only real government in much of Pennsylvania. Back-country dissidents joined Philadelphia radicals to demand a popularly elected constitutional convention, insisting that the Assembly was a mere legislature without any constituent powers. As a horrified aristocracy sulked, and as the Assembly disintegrated, the popular elements carefully screened the voters by loyalty oaths and elected a convention with heavy western representation. Only a few intellectuals, such as Franklin and Rittenhouse, gave it respectability. Former outsiders, restive and near-illiterate westerners, and young men inspired by Thomas Paine drafted a declaration of rights and a very original plan of government with a unicameral legislature. The convention also made an unprecedented attempt to give meaning to popular sovereignty.

In Pennsylvania, unlike almost every other state, the successful demand for a convention accompanied a major shift in political power. Without any formal redefinition of franchise rules, local committees not only excluded suspected loyalists but also permitted unpropertied militiamen to vote. Perhaps the resulting convention was not more representative, but it did reflect an equalitarian shift and gave more voice to the lower classes than did those in any other colony. The delegates celebrated popular sovereignty but did not always understand the concept. They confused it with democracy. The plan of government required equal apportionment, accountability in voting (open sessions, a published journal, and roll call votes), and made the people part of the legislative process. The Assembly was to print all bills of a public nature for public perusal and discussion and, except on "occasions of sudden necessity," defer final passage until after an election. In fact, "sudden necessity" usually prevailed. But the intent was clear. More than ever before, the people, or at least effective majorities, were to rule.[6]

The Pennsylvania convention faced up to a difficult question: How insure compliance by government to the exact terms of a compact? Even the Delaware amendment provision hardly solved this problem. Pennsylvania tried to solve it with a clumsy but ingenious Council of Censors to be elected every seven years by the voters of the state. The council represented a continuing constitutional process, and one clearly distinct from ordinary legislation. It was, first of all, a review body, with a one-year tenure in which to investigate the record of the existing government to insure that it had preserved the constitution intact in every part, and had not exceeded allocated powers or failed as "guardians of the people." This review required a virtual audit of state finances. The council was also an amending device. If defects appeared in the constitution, if amendments appeared necessary, the council could call a constitutional convention. Six months before delegate selection, it had to present for public review all proposed amendments, insuring fully instructed delegates.[7]

The Council of Censors functioned only once in Pennsylvania (see pp. 171–72). The 1776 constitution, always a center of controversy both as to its content and its mode of adoption, gave way in 1790 to a new constitution modeled on those in most other states. It did not even have an amendment provision. But in 1777, little Vermont, struggling to get independence from New York as well as from Britain, virtually copied the Pennsylvania constitution. There the Council of Censors functioned until 1870. The councils recommended major constitutional changes in 1793, 1828, and 1836, including the addition of an upper house and veto powers for the governor. In 1869, meeting for the last time, the council successfully recommended new amendment procedures and deletion of the section that provided for the council. It committed suicide. Long before this meeting the courts had assumed the task of constitutional review, and almost all the states had simpler amendment provisions.[8]

None of the other 1776 conventions struggled so ardently to give meaning to popular sovereignty. A popularly elected Maryland convention completed a declaration of rights (modeled on Virginia's) and a constitution in November 1776. In recognition of the logic of popular sovereignty, several local districts informally relaxed the normal franchise requirements, thus permitting almost all adult males a voice in the delegate selection. The final document did set one important precedent—a simple amendment provision that allowed a popular input. The legislature was to propose amendments, publish them for public discussion, and finally ratify them only after an election.[9]

Influenced by John Adams' "Thoughts on Government," and indebted to Virginia, the North Carolina Assembly, by the terms of a popular mandate, established a constitution in December 1776. It did not provide for amendments and completely failed to follow procedures suggested by the largely Presbyterian and Baptist counties of Orange and Mecklenburg. These dissenting and outspoken Calvinists, who ably upheld their political heritage on many occasions, distinguished the superior power in the people and the inferior power of governments created by them. What the people order at the superior level cannot be altered by the inferior. They vainly asked for popular ratification, a privilege first attained by fellow Calvinists in Massachusetts and New Hampshire.[10]

Georgia and New York completed constitutions in 1777, but made no important innovations in the area of popular sovereignty. An insecure New York convention, after several moves and suspended sessions, failed even to provide for amendment.[11] Georgia began a flurry of constitutional activity in 1777. Its original constitution provided for a clumsy amendment process—a petition for a new convention by a majority of voters in a majority of countries. Because of popular demands, a new convention met in 1789 to draft a new constitution; a second met to ratify it; and, by the terms of the constitution, a third met to review it in 1794. The review convention not only added major amendments but also provided for another review in 1797. This final review convention, surely out of sheer constitutional fatigue, proposed a more stable constitution with simple amendment procedures.[12]

The last of the original state constitutions—in Massachusetts—was by far the most significant, not only in its later influence on the federal constitution but also because of its full compliance with the logic of popular sovereignty. When Massachusetts ousted British authority in 1774 it had to improvise its government. In 1775 the Massachusetts House chose members of an upper house or council, and thus set up an extralegal General Court or Provincial Congress. The congress claimed the rights of the old, 1629 charter, which provided for an elected governor. With the Declaration of Independence the reliance on a resurrected charter lost much of its appeal, for the king had issued the charter. In the eyes of many citizens, Massachusetts in 1776 had no legal government and by the well-accepted canons of popular sovereignty could not have one without a new convention. Since the congress governed without rightful authority, some recalcitrant western counties threatened secession. Even the congress accepted the necessity of some type of constitutional action, some strategy to get out of what some considered a state of nature. In 1776 it asked the towns for authority to draft a constitution. Most towns granted it, but nine, including Boston, denied such powers to a legislative body and demanded a special convention. At least one town also asked for popular ratification and another for full manhood suffrage on constitutional issues.

The congress refused to surrender its initiative. It asked the people in their annual May elections to authorize the new congress to draft a compact for submission to the towns, with final ratification only by vote of two-thirds of all adult males. It tried, in other words, to finesse a special convention by honoring the by then widely demanded right of popular ratification. Despite continued protests against mixing legislative and constituent processes, the towns elected their representatives by the existing suffrage. The congress submitted its draft in December 1777. The towns, with all adult males legally voting for the first time in American history, rejected it. Some towns denied authority to a legislative body. Many saw the constitution as a means for those already in power to retain it. Others, enamored of the Pennsylvania constitution, rejected specific provisions, such as that for a powerful governor. The voluminous objections and recommendations sent back to Boston showed how well even the common people understood the nuances of political theory. By now it was clear that, if Massachusetts were to have a compact at all, it would clearly have to be a popular one in all respects.

The Provincial Congress had no option except a constitutional convention. By a three-to-one margin, the people approved such a convention in 1779. The towns elected the same number of delegates as they had to the General Court, but once again suspended normal suffrage requirements. The convention, the first in history based on such a broad suffrage, met on September 1, 1779. John Adams prepared an early draft and exerted by far the most influence on the final document. It had a distinct declaration of rights and a complex plan of government. In form, it departed in several ways from earlier compacts and exerted influence on almost every subsequent charter. Instead of routine amendment procedures (Adams included none in his draft), the final draft stipulated a review convention in 1795 if two-thirds of the towns desired it. The first amending convention met in 1820. According to the terms of its appointment, the 1779 convention had to submit the draft to the towns for article-by-article review. It received back a confusing mass of deletions and proposed amendments. Only by a tricky tabulation was the convention able to declare the constitution adopted by the two-thirds of the towns. After a confusing six years in the constitutional wilderness, Massachusetts finally had a legal government.[13]

Massachusetts met every procedural requirement remotely implied by popular sovereignty. It elected a special convention, by universal suffrage, to draft a preliminary covenant for submission to, and approval by, the people in the towns. It recognized their continuing sovereignty by a requirement of periodic review (changed in 1820 to amendment procedures). In fact, it took the idea of popular ratification to a rare extreme. The article-by-article review in each town meeting made individual citizens participants in the drafting of the final document. In the federal Constitution, in most states, the right of popular ratification would mean only a popular referendum.

In Massachusetts the problem of franchise joined with the issue of popular sovereignty. Even in Massachusetts, the lair of Puritan theory, some radicals used the rhetoric of popular sovereignty to advocate full manhood suffrage in all areas, not just on constituent processes. Their logic was faulty, but their appeal would eventually succeed. Of all the states, only Massachusetts recognized that the difference between constitutional and legislative process demanded separate suffrage requirements. Thus, in Massachusetts, all adult males ratified a constitution which excluded many of them from the subsequent franchise by means of property requirements. But if the people were really sovereign, they had a right to set up a monarchy with no elections if they so desired. In their original constitutions every state set at least minimal economic limits on the franchise, ranging from small tax requirements in Pennsylvania and Georgia to freehold requirements in Rhode Island and Virginia. These requirements, as they applied to ordinary governmental processes, have no significance for popular sovereignty. But in each state except Massachusetts the existing franchise also governed the constitutional process. However mild the franchise limitations, however few people excluded, the resulting constitutions did not rest on the "whole" people. Even in subsequent constitutional revisions, the states would not relax normal suffrage requirements. Virginia even refused, in her ratification requirements, to relax freehold requirements to the extent provided in the proposed new constitution of 1830. Two states—Connecticut and New York—did broaden the suffrage for ratifying the federal Constitution, but not because of allegiance to principle. Only the widespread adoption of universal manhood suffrage in the nineteenth century made these distinctions moot.

At the federal level the first clear compact of government was the federal Constitution of 1787. The Articles of Confederation was neither fish nor fowl. The state governments, not the people, established it. No clarifying theory informed its ratification. Article II affirmed the sovereignty of each confederated state, a statement that could mean either of two things: That the people of each state retained their sovereignty, and thus their right to bestow sovereign powers on such local or federated governments as they wanted; or it could mean, and clearly so suggested, that the state governments were the constituents of the Articles, and that it was only a treaty or alliance of these governments. In conformity with the second interpretation, and despite broad powers, the confederated government usually operated through the state governments and not directly upon the people.

The Articles provided for a type of amendment, subject to the agreement of the legislatures and not the people of every state (again the mark of a treaty). In theory, the Constitutional Convention of 1787 convened under this authority. Therefore, the state governments correctly appointed the delegates. Nothing in the selection process foretold the end product, which was rather clearly a compact of government. It claimed the authority of the people even though they never authorized the convention. Only the terms of ratification—by special conventions in each state—at all fulfilled the claim, and arrested the nagging doubts of many delegates that they had any legal or moral right to draft such a constitution.

The federal convention left ambiguous all issues of sovereignty. The delegates neither agreed nor even remained individually consistent on these issues. The Preamble declared that "We, the people of the United States" ordained and established the Constitution. But even this phraseology contained a fatal ambiguity. Did it mean that the sovereign people in each state, upon ratification, joined in establishing a common government to which they delegated certain of their sovereign powers? Or did it mean that the heretofore sovereign people of an individual state, upon ratification, gave up their sovereignty, their separate existence as a nation, and became part of one large commonwealth, and in this context jointly exercised their sovereignty in apportioning certain powers to their national government? Either of these interpretations honors the unity and indivisibility of sovereignty. The trouble is that no one at the convention clarified these alternatives.

The convention wrestled with other semantic confusions. Words such as *confederation, federation,* and *national* also had no precise connotations. In the convention, delegates usually used *federal* to designate an alliance of sovereign states, and contrasted it with a *national* system, or a single sovereign entity with subordinate political subdivisions. It is ironic that the "nationalists" within the convention later assumed the title of "federalists," and the convention "federalists" gained the misleading title of "antifederalists." Much later, John C. Calhoun offered precise definitions of all these terms in defense of his claim that the convention did create a federal government. Calhoun's definitions did not help the delegates at Philadelphia. One can only guess how they would have fitted their achievement to his analytical categories.

Calhoun defined a *confederation* as an alliance of the governments of nation states. The United States was such a confederation until 1789. A *federation*, in contrast, is a union of sovereign states based upon a popular compact. The sovereign people of a state (correctly used, *state* attaches only to a sovereign entity) compact certain powers of sovereignty to a local government, and certain others to a federal or common government. Since the powers, in each case, rest on the sovereign people, the governments are coordinate in rank and mutually exclusive in power. If the people of a state so desire, they may grant very sweeping powers to a federal government and very little jurisdiction to their local government. The critical point is that each government is inferior to the sovereign will of the people of a state. The people may recompact at will, either to change the form of their local government or to recommend to other states basic changes in the federal government (since other states adhere to the federal system by their own compacts, or by ratification of a common compact, a single commonwealth cannot unilaterally change the federal government). If they are unable to get essential amendments in the federal government, the people of a state always retain the right to reclaim all the sovereign powers they granted to the federal government, either to vest them in their local government or in another federation. Even as they bestow such powers by solemn convenant, so must they retrieve them by a constitutional action or by a special convention.

Calhoun believed this model of federalism best reflected the intentions, if not the language, of a vast majority of delegates at Philadelphia. Most did not want to abolish thirteen states and create one large state. They simply wanted an effective federal government and an enduring union. In this retrospective judgment, Calhoun was probably correct. Except for extreme nationalists, such a federal government seems close to what moderates such as Madison or Randolph really desired. They wanted a federal government with exclusive powers in critical areas, resting directly upon the people of the states and no longer dependent on state governments. They might even have accepted the one most disturbing implication of Calhoun's model—secession. Such a model might also have accommodated moderate state righters, such as James Patterson and other friends of the small states, who had no desire to maintain a weak federal government, or even George Mason, who feared for civil liberties under an overly centralized system. Only a Luther Martin, a partisan of the confederation and of the prerogatives of state governments, would have found Calhoun's model too nationalistic.

But a few delegates wanted something more nationalistic. James Wilson of Pennsylvania and Alexander Hamilton of New York wanted a national government, not Calhoun's strong version of a federal one. As Calhoun saw it, a unified national government was the sole agent of one sovereign people. If the Constitution achieved such a government, it effected a constitutional revolution by converting the former states into political subdivisions. But there is here an alternative not clearly grasped by Calhoun. In a unified state he assumed all except one government would be subordinate. Not of necessity. As European advocates of popular sovereignty made clear, the sovereign people of a large commonwealth may desire several coordinate governments, each with exclusive powers in specified areas. The sovereign people of America, as one people, could severely restrict the powers of a national government and reserve vast powers to several local governments. The powers, in both cases, would be recallable by the people. If New York gained its local governmental powers, not from the sovereign people of New York (no such commonwealth exists) but from the sovereign people of the nation, its powers were no less secure from usurpation by the national government. But the people of the nation could retract what they bestowed; in becoming part of a larger whole, New York would lose its claim to autonomous constitutional processes. It could not secede by right. But so long as the sovereign people of the whole nation chose to delegate broad powers and privileges to local governments, by *compact and not by grant* of a central government, then America did have a form of federalism. (Althusius and others had long used the word for commonwealths with such complex levels of government.)

Wilson and Hamilton wanted just this form of federalism. At the Pennsylvania ratifying convention Wilson not only defended the new federal system but also gave the clearest analysis of sovereignty of anyone in America before Calhoun. He based his whole defense on the complete sovereignty of the American people, and over and over again stressed that they could apportion the powers of government as they wished. He rejected the contention of critics that the new Constitution represented a consolidation of sovereignty. Unlike Calhoun, he believed that the Declaration of Independence created one "great community" containing many lesser communities. The Articles reflected an early and mistaken choice of that great community to place most governmental powers in the states. The new Constitution, without significantly reducing the functions of the state governments, now placed many new powers in the central government. This shift did not touch the location of sovereignty, which remained in the whole body of people. Hamilton did not make the same analytical distinctions. In his infrequent attendance at the convention, he argued strongly against leaving the states "in possession of their Sovereignty." But he also confessed that the amazing extent of the country discouraged any "general sovereignty." Caught in semantic traps, he rejected overly subtle reasoning and defined a "federal government" as the "association of independent communities into one," leaving optional the range and extent of centralized governmental power.[14]

Lacking analytical tools to express their views on sovereignty, most of the delegates at Philadelphia floundered in verbal confusion. Gunning Bedford of Delaware saw only dilemmas. There was, he believed, no middle way. Either the delegates created a perfect consolidation or continued a confederation of states, equally if "not perfectly" sovereign. He did not explain the "not perfectly," and made a common identification between sovereignty and government, a fatal error for anyone desiring to understand the American federal system. A cautious Madison pointed to existing "limits" on state sovereignty (here he obviously meant limits on state governments, and not on the ultimate prerogative of the people of a state), and found in the developing Constitution only an increase in such limits. George Mason said the new federal government would have a "qualified sovereignty" only, while the individual states retained a part of their sovereignty. His was one of many suggestions of divided sovereignty (meaning, in most cases, a division of the powers of sovereignty, and thus more of a contradiction in language than in meaning). Perhaps the puzzled Elbridge Gerry best summed up the confusion: "We are in a peculiar situation. We were neither the same Nation nor different Nations." The logic of the situation, as he saw it, was to find a footing somewhere in the interstices between two equally untenable positions.[15]

Although unsure of which people possessed sovereignty, a majority of the delegates reaffirmed its location in "the people." They also aligned federal constitutional processes with those already established in the states. The issue came to the fore in a relatively restricted debate over the means of ratification. At least a sprinkling of delegates, including Oliver Ellsworth and James Patterson, supported ratification by state legislatures. For Patterson, this method was consistent with his support of small-state equality and his loyalty to many features of the confederation. Only Elbridge Gerry of Massachusetts denigrated the new-fangled idea of popular conventions. He sought legislative ratification as called for by the Articles but wanted to suspend the requirement of unanimity. Rufus King, although in favor of popular ratification as a means of establishing the legitimacy of a new government, still argued the legality of the amending provision in the Articles. Tacit consent, popular acquiescence, had certified this mode of amendment.[16]

Such heresy invited a barrage of counterarguments, many rooted in principle. George Mason pointed out that state legislatures were only creatures of state constitutions, and had no power competent to such constituent action. To submit to legislatures was also to invite future amendments by them. That only the people had such power was the very basis of free government. To the consternation of other delegates, he further alleged the incompetence of some state legislatures, his own in Virginia included, because they had not received their power from the "clear & undisputed authority of the people." On more practical grounds, John Randolph favored popular ratification in order to establish the superiority of the federal over state governments, a position that appealed to most nationalists. Gouverneur Morris believed only an appeal to popular sovereignty could bypass the unanimity principle in the Articles. Madison gave the broadest support to popular ratification, mixing his practical commitment to a strong national government with appeals to principle. He dismissed as "novel & dangerous" the doctrine that legislatures could change the very constitution that gave them existence. The true difference between a league or treaty and a constitutional government was the voice of the people. He used the law of nations (possibly Vattel) to vindicate his position. Only three small states voted for legislative ratification;

only one—Maryland—voted against a later motion to refer to
the people of the states.[17]

One final clause, Article V on amendments, concerned popular sovereignty. Unfortunately, it came up so late in the convention that it received very little attention or discussion. The
article, both in an original draft and in final form, violated popular sovereignty, for it allowed amendments solely by legislative
action. George Mason, by then the watchdog of popular sovereignty, secured a small change in the original plan after vainly
pleading that no amendment of the proper kind could ever "be
obtained by the people, if the Government should become oppressive." The original plan allowed two-thirds of the state legislatures, as well as the federal Congress, to propose amendments
for final ratification by three-fourths of the states. As amended,
the state legislatures could only secure a convention to make
such proposals, thus providing one mechanism for popular participation. In actual fact, the other path has prevailed; all
amendments have come through congressional proposals and
state ratification. The people have had no direct role in the
amendment process.[18]

In a few brief years, 1776 to 1789, the principle of popular
sovereignty matured in America into enduring institutions. The
one unsettled question at the beginning of our national period
was how the people could ever force governments to adhere to
their compacts. The Councils of Censors in Pennsylvania and in
Vermont reflected one cumbersome answer at the state level.
Soon, at both the state and federal levels, the courts would claim
the primary responsibility for constitutional review. Their eventual success in winning broad popular acceptance for this claim
marked an unwritten accretion to our constitutions that rivaled
in importance the development of a two-party system.

A special constitutional responsibility for the courts reflected
the necessary logic of popular sovereignty. But in no sense did
popular sovereignty mandate the degree of later constitutional
deference paid to the Supreme Court by other branches of government or by the people. In part, this deference reflected the

need for some orderly way of settling divisive constitutional issues. In part, it reflected the achievements of able and strong judges. John Marshall's dramatic claim in *Marbury* v. *Madison* followed a few rather clear precedents at the state level. The infrequent use of the weapon by the United States Supreme Court also smoothed the way for popular acceptance. Such constitutional review was a break with aspects of the British legal system. Not that English judges avoided constitutional issues. Far from it. But England lacked a separate constitutional process. Parliament was the final court of appeal as well as the supreme legislator. In this context, the lower courts might interpret and apply legislation but could not finally overturn it. A higher body, capable of overruling Parliament, made no sense and, in the tradition of Locke and Blackstone, threatened the very essence of sovereignty—the supremacy of legislative power. But in the tradition of Vattel, and even of some English radical theorists, it made perfect sense. The fundamental law, the terms of the compact, constitutes a form of law and thus a necessary component of judicial decision. If one accepted popular sovereignty, then clearly the fundamental law took precedence over the mere acts of a dependent legislature. Even when a representative legislature exceeded its delegated powers by the emphatic consent of an overwhelming majority of the people, their matured will as expressed in a solemn convenant still took precedence over the whims of the moment. If their new desires had enduring appeal, they could effect them through constitutional revision.

At Philadelphia only two delegates explicitly referred to judicial review. Their remarks allow no judgment about the views of the majority. Luther Martin argued against judicial participation in legislative review (the veto power of the president) because the same judges would have a later right of veto when they ruled on the constitutionality of laws. George Mason, quite consistent with his concern over popular sovereignty, accepted Martin's contention. He noted only that judicial review negated existing, clearly unconstitutional laws, but allowed judges no leeway in enforcing pernicious yet constitutional measures. Their wisdom in legislative review might prevent bad laws as well as unconstitutional ones.[19]

Hamilton, in *The Federalist* no. 78, offered the fullest argument for judicial review and also left the impression that such a role had been a common assumption in the convention (James Wilson used similar arguments at the Pennsylvania ratifying convention). Hamilton was always a fervent defender of both natural rights and popular sovereignty. As others who feared majoritarian democracy, he gladly conceded the ultimate power of the people to decide on their form of government, and hoped they would not only choose wisely but that they would be satisfied with this ultimate but usually residual authority. For men of the view of Hamilton or John Adams, an appointed, independent, life-tenured, honored, and well-paid judiciary provided the one most likely area of responsible government, in part because it was nonelective and nonresponsive. Hamilton believed the Supreme Court would pose the least threat to the rights granted by the Constitution. The executive had the sword. The Congress had the purse. The judges had only wisdom. Only judges were in a position to enforce constitutional limitations upon the executive and the legislature. It was the duty of the Court "to declare all acts contrary to the manifest tenor of the Constitution void. Without this, all the reservations of particular rights or privileges would amount to nothing." To disarm a lingering suspicion of any power superior to a representative legislature, Hamilton simply stressed the status of fundamental law. In interpreting it the courts are an intermediary between the sovereign people and a limited legislature. Judges have to interpret the meaning of the fundamental law as well as statutory law. In all cases of conflict the intentions of the people take precedence over the intentions of their agents.[20]

As even Hamilton conceded, judges should always seek a fair interpretation in order to reconcile fundamental and statutory law. Judicial review, which allows interpretive leeway, should not provide judges with legislative powers. Even with all due restraint, a judge may still have to decide between two conflicting laws at two levels of authority. To make such a decision is a strictly judicial function, and an inescapable one if justice is to be done. The courts thus check legislative will and beyond that the momentary whims and fancies of a people, or what Hamilton called their "occasional ill humors." For Hamilton, judicial review was an instrument of continuity, of ordered procedures, of secure liberties, of stability. It upheld the mature, dispassionate, traditional wisdom of a people as interred in their most solemn covenants. Thus, the least democratic branch of government was nonetheless the prime defender of the people's ultimate sovereignty, even as democratic legislatures always posed the greatest threat to it.[21]

Few would disagree with Hamilton's main contention—judges must give precedence to constitutional law and in order to do so must be able to block the enforcement of what they perceive as clearly unconstitutional legislation. But few Americans were so sanguine about judges. The old doctrine of legislative sovereignty would never gain significant American supporters, either in Congress or in the courts. Even the later, fervent advocates of judicial restraint always acknowledged the necessity of a court veto over blatantly unconstitutional legislation. But at the political level constitutional review by the courts has often stimulated intense opposition, either by aggrieved political leaders or by angry majorities. The will of the majority has often seemed self-justifying, and the obstructions of judges a throwback to earlier forms of arrogant aristocracy. This mood, for it rarely has bloomed into a full theory, has surfaced during popular crusades (as in New Deal efforts to circumvent the existing Supreme Court judges) or whenever an activist Court has so interpreted the Constitution as to force rapid and frightening social changes.

The doctrine of popular sovereignty requires a higher level of constitutional law, limits the power of all legislatures, and adds a new dimension to judicial process. But it also denies sovereignty to all branches of government. A court with full authority to resolve constitutional issues would represent a new form of governmental sovereignty. Thus, from the perspective of popular sovereignty, the necessary function of court construction must never be confused with a final power to determine what is or is not constitutional. Only the people can make this decision. In carrying out their tasks, all public officials have a sworn obligation to uphold the Constitution. At the federal level, Congress has the obligation to legislate within the bounds set by the Constitution. The president must adhere to delegated powers, and is under obligation to veto any legislation that, in his best judgment, is unconstitutional. The import of these obligations is clear: the Supreme Court may refuse to enforce legislation but does not thereby determine canons of constitutionality for the other two branches or for the people as a whole unless they are willing to follow the logic of its decisions. A Congress or a president always has a right to disagree with a Court's constitutional rulings. They have an equal duty with judges to make clear their interpretations. They may challenge the Court by continuing to pass legislation in line with their interpretation, either in behalf of interim enforcement or in hopes of more enlightened judges. Favorable Court decisions in no sense diminish the constitutional responsibility of Congress and the president. As Andrew Jackson so forcibly argued in his veto of Court-approved internal improvements and a federally chartered bank, he had the sworn responsibility of upholding the Constitution as he understood it, not as a few misguided Supreme Court judges had formerly interpreted it.

Even these qualifications on judicial review at the federal level left unresolved some disturbing dilemmas noted by thoroughgoing advocates of popular sovereignty. These dilemmas soon seemed most live and important in the South, or in a region that often had compelling reasons to dissent from federal policy. Even if all three branches of the federal government share the responsibility of constitutional review, they may all concur in an unconstitutional expansion of federal power. They may agree on such an implausible construction of key sections of the Constitution as to change its basic meaning, and by so doing turn the federal government into a sovereign entity, since power over constitutional process is the substance of sovereignty. Such a power grab poses the greatest possible threat to a constitutional federation, for by illegitimate means the existing federal government effectively destroys the charter commitments and guarantees that led the people of certain states to ratify the Constitution and become a participant in the union. In such a context, amendment procedures are of no more avail than appeals to a subverted Court. The same usurping federal Congress has the initiating role in the simplest amending procedure, and the more cumbersome technique—a new constitutional convention—requires the unlikely support of two-thirds of the state legislatures.

Of course, if the people of individual states are sovereign, they always have a right to withdraw their ratification of the federal compact. Southern leaders rarely questioned state sovereignty, but they desperately sought remedies short of secession and a disrupted union. All their strategies, from the Virginia and Kentucky Resolutions of Madison and Jefferson to Calhoun's theories about nullification, involved some counterbalancing constitutional role for the states. Jefferson articulated very well the belief that the states were the prime interpreters of the federal compact. A sovereign state had a "natural right" to nullify any violation of a compact, else it was under the dominion of an absolute and unlimited federal power. At times he even gloried in the possibilities of popular constitutional revolt. But it was John Taylor of Caroline County, Virginia, who offered the most careful and balanced argument for a major state role in constitutional interpretation.

Taylor stressed that the federal Constitution, a compact ratified by the sovereign people of each state, not only delegated certain powers of sovereignty to the federal government, but also placed certain restrictions on state governments even as it reserved a broad spectrum of powers for the states. Thus, state officials as much as federal came under the federal Constitution and rightly swore to uphold it. But to uphold it, they too had to interpret its meaning. If the interpretation of state legislators or state judges differed from that of federal officials, particularly on crucial jurisdictional issues, then there was a constitutional impasse at least comparable to that occasioned by constitutional disagreements among the branches of government. Taylor emphasized that both state and federal officials had an equal or co-ordinate responsibility and authority to interpret the document. Only sheer power, not right, would permit one side to impose its interpretation on the other. If a state legislature or a state court tried to impose its eccentric interpretation on federal officials, then conscientious officials should ignore it and continue to enforce existing federal laws. Likewise, state officials should interpose their legislation or court rulings to block enforcement of what they interpreted as unconstitutional federal action.

Obviously, such mutual interposition threatened some form of legal chaos. Taylor preferred this disorder to tyranny. He recommended mutual accommodation for minor controversies and an early recourse to amendment procedures for serious ones. His purpose, so close to later recommendations by Calhoun, was clear—to force the use of slow and cumbersome constitutional processes to vindicate any major shift in the relative powers of state or federal governments. Otherwise, aggrieved minorities would later have to use such processes in almost inevitably futile efforts to reverse an illegal *fait accompli*. The early use of constitutional procedures not only met the requirements of popular sovereignty but also insured something closer to a national consensus and forced a greater effort to accommodate minority interests in any final resolution of conflict.

ⓒⓒⓒ

PART TWO

4. *The Legal and Moral Heritage*

T HEORIES ABOUT NATURAL LAW and right are as old as Western civilization, and constitute perhaps the most persistent strain in Western moral theory. The basic premise is beguilingly simple: that without special revelation, or commands of any sort, or any threat of punishment, thoughtful and reasonable men can still recognize inescapable duties and obligations. These responsibilities are inherent in the human situation, in the world as it is, in man as he is, and in the ends or purposes that attach to both.

But the seeming simplicity of natural-law theories is deceptive. The mere affirmation of a universal moral order leaves the difficult problem not only of vindicating its lawful status but also of defining its specific terms. In the West the vindications and definitions have varied immensely. At the same time, ambiguities of language have confused both the statement and the understanding of the theories. For modern man, the rhetoric of natural law and natural rights is peculiarly archaic, for it contains very subtle, contextually qualified, and increasingly neglected uses for such elusive words as *nature, reason, right,* and *law.*

Today the word *law* has at least a twofold meaning. In a physical context it denotes necessary behavioral regularities. This meaning is only tangentially related to theories of natural right, for this type of law is beyond human choice although available for consultation and guidance. In a moral or political context, law denotes obligatory standards. In this second or normative sense law implies purposeful agents and end-directed behavior. Lawful conduct contributes to some desired end—to peace, or justice, or happiness. But, unfortunately for perfect clarity, the desired ends may only be those of the lawgiver. A law is in all cases a rule of conduct, but it may be such as a manifestation of sheer power rather than as a moral code. In a moral perspective one may acknowledge only those laws which contribute to what one perceives as a good end, such as the glory of God or greater human happiness. But, obviously, some people use the word *law* preeminently, or even exclusively, for legislated and enforced rules, or for the positive law of a state. Fortunately for the peace of mind of most people, the two senses of law are not exclusive. A state may enact and enforce the very rules that one perceives as morally obligatory. But if it does not, then one has a dilemma—which category of law to obey.

The same ambiguity applies to the word *right.* From the perspective of duty a law compels behavior; from the perspective of right it allows behavior. If a law—moral or positive—sanctions private property, then one has a right to possess such property. But right may only mean that one is at liberty to possess such property, and not that it is good, or morally right, for anyone to have private property. Perhaps even more than the word *law,* the word *right* suggests a moral connotation, and in the tradition of natural rights always possessed that meaning, in part because of the very root meaning of the word *right* and also because of the qualification given it by the word *natural.*

That only invites a much more difficult question: What gives to a law or a right the status of "natural"? Such a question begs further definition, particularly of two of the most ambiguous words in our language—*nature* and *reason*. Natural-law theories originated in Greek philosophy. Plato and Aristotle affirmed not only a formal logical order in the world but also an inherent purposefulness in all things. Nature stood for both the order and the purpose. Aristotle's universe was one vast congeries of yearnings, of informed objects moving toward their own perfection and, in a sense, trying to imitate the objects above them in a chain of being stretching to a perfect mind which pulls all things toward it. Man, by his intellect, can grasp the formal truth in objects, can understand the structure of the universe. More important, he can understand himself, grasp his own nature, which is also to perceive his own highest good. Aristotle defined this highest good as a form of happiness, and related it to life in the polis, the most inclusive human community. Politics is the practical art that man uses to seek happiness in this most inclusive form of public life.

In a context of inherent purpose, natural law has a normative and not a mechanical meaning. Even for nonintelligent objects, the important law is that which properly relates an object to its end, to its highest perfection, to its proper function in the whole scheme of things. In man this law works not at the level of tendency or even instinct, but at the level of apprehension and thought, for the distinctive, essential attribute of man is intelligence, or reason. Any good polis, believed Aristotle, will be governed by objective and humane laws, by what mature wisdom has disclosed. Thus, in words that Cicero made famous, the law of nature for man is the voice of right reason, even as nature is reason objectified. For Cicero, and for earlier Stoics, who first popularized the distinctive language of natural law and celebrated the reason in nature, the word *reason* stood at the convergence of taste, logic, and empirical knowledge, of intuitive apprehension, correct deductions, and science. By appeal to such reason, one can decipher the universal principles of correct behavior, the moral laws that are rooted, not in arbitrary will or local circumstances or sheer power, but in reality itself.

Greek concepts of inherent purpose, of a hierarchy of essence, reflected a very sophisticated anthropomorphizing of reality, an objectification of the experienced world by concepts appropriate to intelligent organisms. But such a view did not require a belief in theistic design. For Aristotle, lawfulness and purpose inhered in a reality that was, itself, eternal and in no sense the product of creative intelligence. But nonetheless this Greek view of a purposeful reality was easily assimilated by early Christians, and became a vital part of Christian theology. The Hebrews, with all their moralism, and despite their elaborate legal system, did not have a theory of natural law (this does not preclude much of their Mosaic law from meeting natural-law requirements as men later defined them). The Jews perceived their law, not as inherent in nature and open to right reason, but as the direct command of Jehovah. By a later, Greek-inspired Christian view, a divine and benevolent creator implanted at least part of His law in the created world and bestowed on man the intellectual faculties necessary to apprehend this inherent law, thus making it available to all mankind and not exclusively available to recipients of a special and direct revelation. In fact, the idea of a divine intelligence, not in Aristotle's sense of an inviting perfection at the most lofty peak of reality, but as the author of all law, provided a welcome sanction for natural-law theories. Cicero, an eclectic, non-Christian theist, saw God as both author and enforcing judge of natural law. Since God promulgated natural law and embedded it in nature, no man can be exempt from its eternal and unchangeable commands, no legitimate government can alter it, and anyone who even tries to revise or repeal it commits a sin.[1]

The only scriptural support for natural law came from Paul, a student of Stoicism. He informed the Romans: "When Gentiles who do not possess the law [of Moses] carry out its precepts by the light of nature, then, although they have no law, they are their own law, for they display the effect of the law inscribed on their hearts." [2] But the scriptural support was hardly necessary. Natural-law theories informed Roman jurisprudence, were already commonplace by the fourth century, and would remain so through the Middle Ages. Natural law always made up at least one category of law, and coexisted with divine revelation or divine positive law and with human positive law, or the laws of the state based on command and fitted to local circumstances. And the only positive law that could claim legitimacy had to be consistent, in principle, with divine and natural law.

Natural law transcends the problems of government. No government is its source. Even without a government men are under its obligation. Despite government, or even contrary to it, they remain subject to it. Seneca, the Roman Stoic, realized that a law of nature implies a "state of nature," meaning a human community governed only by principles of right reason. Seneca believed such a state had existed in an earlier, innocent age in which men held all things in common and lived peacefully with each other. Greed, vice, and the tyranny of sheer power later forced men to form governments. For Seneca, as for many of his successors all the way to the present, coercive political authority seemed an "unnatural," even if necessary, human contrivance. And his conception of a state of nature remained through the eighteenth century as one of the main conventions of normative political theory. It served well to clarify the minimal, moral ends of government, for no one would voluntarily leave a state of nature if he did not believe that a social order would better protect his rights.

Even more than conceptions of popular sovereignty, natural law remained at the heart of medieval political theory. God ordained government, gave His authority to it, and allowed the people of a community to choose the exact form of government. But God ordained, and people should consent, only in behalf of thoroughly moral ends, in behalf of justice, happiness, or the general welfare. These essential ends, given specific form, are men's natural rights. The universal rules of conduct necessary to attain them constitute natural law, a law binding as much on the governors as on the governed. Beyond this natural law there was divine law as revealed in scripture or through the Church, and below it there was locally varied customary and positive law. Medieval theorists gave to tradition, to the cherished habits of a people, almost as much sanction as universal principles of right. They often resisted ideas of legislation, even as they resisted the modern, centralized, sovereign state. Princes and parliaments should clarify, promulgate, and interpret law, not make it. Even positive law was, at best, only the application of natural law to peculiar, local conditions.[3]

Because of the long, deductive path from abstract principles to specific legislation, natural-law theories could, in practice, lend moral legitimacy to almost any legal system. In England, Coke and other jurists used it to provide a higher sanction for the common law, for a system of law common to the whole realm and which developed out of ancient custom, monarchical decree, court decisions, and, eventually, parliamentary "clarifications." Since natural law constituted, at best, a body of moral principles, it did not provide a ready-made body of universally binding statutes, but rather provided a standard of criticism for evaluating legislation. Judged by universal principles of justice, a monarchical edict might appear arbitrary and, in a moral sense, "illegal" if it thwarted rather than furthered the minimal ends of government.

The Reformation added nothing new to natural-law theories, but soon added a special urgency to minority appeals to natural rights. Calvin and Luther reinforced the natural-law tradition. Calvin, like Aquinas, defined natural law as the branch of divine law inherent in the created order and apparent to man before the fall of Adam. It remained, in principle, knowable by all men, or present to "men of all nations and times. . . ." But Calvin appreciated the difficulties sinful men had in attaining right reason, and how often they disagreed on the exact content of natural law. It was so easy for men to bend natural law to their own will and desire, or to appeal to it in cases where it did not fit. In an age of clashing religious beliefs Calvin appreciated the most telling practical weakness of natural-law theory—it works well as a moral embellishment of consensual views and established customs in a unified society, but too easily becomes a contentious propaganda weapon for rival factions in a divided, heterogeneous society. Calvin and many of his successors, including the English Puritans, preferred the clarity and security of revealed law, and used it whenever possible in their communities. Some extreme Puritans so imitated the scriptures as to leave small room for any law based on right reason. But Calvin was practical enough, or modern enough, to see the need for a great deal of contextual, positive law. Scripture and natural law set limits but do not provide, by simple deduction, all the necessary laws for a state. The called magistrate should be a skilled legislator. Both Luther and Calvin helped expand the legislative function of the state through their rejection of overt political roles for the Church, their attack upon canon law, and their concern for a carefully disciplined and outwardly righteous society.[4]

In the religious wars beleaguered Protestant minorities always paralleled appeals to natural rights with claims of popular sovereignty. Only because of rank injustice, of "arbitrary" and "illegal" acts, could they claim the residual popular right to resist and overturn governments. The Marian exiles, Knox, and Buchanan all defied royal will when they perceived it as contrary to God's will or to the highest form of law, and thus arbitrary and tyrannical. In Britain this appeal to law against royal will was already a venerable tradition. Not so in France. There the radical Huguenots argued that the king, in violating former promises of religious autonomy and in carrying out systematic persecution, had violated almost all their natural rights. Kings, said the author of *Vindiciae*, are appointed as servants for good, to maintain justice, to defend the people from dangers and outrages. He appealed to the logic of the situation. Men consent to a governmental covenant with a king in behalf of assured justice. They would not do that if they knew they were to establish a tyrant, a prince who, on a sudden notion, could cut their throats. No one would consent to having his welfare depend upon another's pleasure. Right should limit might. And note that tyranny is not by definition always some form of harshness or cruelty. It is, above all, arbitrariness or nonlawful government. The Huguenots stressed that a merciful pardon, offered by a monarch contrary to existing law, was as arbitrary and illegal as taking a life without the right to do so.[5]

The Huguenots still followed the Greeks in emphasizing justice as the prime end of a state, but with an unprecedented frequency they also emphasized life and livelihood. In various alternative wordings, they anticipated the later, all too pat, formula of "life, liberty, and property." In *Vindiciae* "the law of nature teaches and commands us to maintain our lives and liberties, without which life is scant worth the enjoying . . ." and "he who questions the lawfulness of defending oneself does, as much as in him lies, question the law of nature." [6] This emphasis upon self-preservation also dated back to the Greeks, and had received almost universal commendation ever since. Some early medieval theorists even used the phrase "law of nature" in a physiological rather than a rational sense—to designate basic, instinctual behavior, such as an animal's effort to preserve its own life. By almost any perspective, the arbitrary, nonlawful taking of life was the clearest possible violation of natural right, even as the preservation and enhancement of life was the clearest single end for a civil society. What seemed new in the Huguenots was a growing sense of an individual autonomy or identity rooted in forms of achievement. This individualism, in part a function of position in society, of the entrepreneurial or free-artisan status of many Huguenot leaders, also reflected Calvinist views of work and property.

Calvin, by his emphasis upon vocations or callings, challenged the existing class system in one vital way—he would countenance no idle leisure class, no aristocracy of luxury, or frivolity, or even piety. At the same time he repudiated prevalent stigmas placed upon types of work. All Christians were to use their God-given talents to the best of their abilities. This emphasis was a double-edged sword. It could dignify all socially beneficial labor and do away with earlier forms of servility. But, slightly distorted, it could give Godly sanction to all existing occupations and encourage servants and wage-laborers to remain content with their lowly tasks and meager pay. The calling doctrine gave new emphasis to an old Christian assumption—that God gave the earth in common to mankind. It was the context for human effort, the clay for man's talents, the stage for his testing. Implicit here were new ideas about property, ideas developed by the Huguenots and given classic statement by John Locke.

The word *property* simply introduces another ambiguity into natural rights. The word had, and still has, many meanings. The early Christian fathers worked out an accommodation with Roman forms of private possession. Still persuaded that common property, as adopted by the early Church, might be the most natural form, they acknowledged that private possession of the means of production and of consumer goods was a practical necessity because of man's selfishness and pride. But the standard of communism remained in monastic orders, or in those situations in which men were able to attain the highest level of obedience. Medieval theorists believed governments should protect legitimate property, with *legitimate* usually meaning such obvious moral criteria as need and actual occupation for land, and expended labor for consumer goods. All purely investment or speculative property remained sinful, as reflected in laws against usury. Aquinas, unlike so many of his Christian progenitors, accepted the state as a natural rather than a conventional institution, but still stopped just short of defining private possessions as natural rights. He believed qualified individual rights to land and goods were supplements to natural rights, necessary adjuncts of organized society, and requirements for maximum economic efficiency. He wanted strict limits, including need and use, and never justified exclusive control. In times of dire need, property once again becomes common. A hungry man can "steal" food without fault. Early Calvinists kept these qualifications, but almost always spoke of property as a natural right.[7]

The author of *Vindiciae* argued that men had property before they had government. It is necessary to livelihood and happiness. Therefore, the people established their monarch in order better to protect, not to steal, that property. He had to protect the poor against the rich, and vice versa. The law of God protects us in our goods, the products of our labor, the "sweat of our brow." At least by implication, the radical Huguenots accepted a labor theory of value. They indicted the king for limiting access to, and profiting from, common salt pits, which, like light, air, and water, nature presented unto men "out of her own bounty" and without human labor, and which therefore should not be for sale.[8] This sense of the earth as a Godly gift, open to wise use and foreclosed to monopolistic control or purely speculative use, remained a Calvinist theme well into the seventeenth century. John Winthrop used a labor theory of value to justify taking Indian lands in North America. The Indians forfeited land by not applying labor to it, or improving it, or finding their vocation on it. The obverse of such a vindication of possession was a losing Puritan effort to restrict land ownership to need, to actual use, with careful regard for the future accessibility of land for immigrants or later generations.

The third conventional end of government—liberty—had a traditional meaning quite easily misunderstood today. It always meant that one was not a slave or, in the perspective of an increasingly despised feudalism, not servile or helplessly dependent on someone else. Literally, the right of liberty was to be at liberty. The whole subject of liberty grew in large part out of the endless medieval debate over slavery and the common Christian acceptance of justifiable slavery only as a substitute for a warranted punishment by death or some other severe penalty. By the American revolution the term *slave*, so often and so endlessly bandied about, denoted almost any degree of involuntary and unjust dependency. It was from this restricted but vital use of *liberty* that a parallel idea of "free and equal" gained distinctive meaning.

Althusius, the German Calvinist, expressed very well the doctrine of human equality, although he said nothing particularly new. He pointed out that, under natural law alone, all men are equally free, for in a state of nature they are not subject to the jurisdiction of anyone else. Locke gave the most influential clarification: natural equality was that *"Equality, which all Men* are in, in respect of Jurisdiction or Dominion one over another . . . , being that *equal Right* that every *Man* hath, to his *Natural Freedom,* without being subjected to the Will or Authority of any other Man." It has, as he noted, nothing to do with age, virtue, excellency of parts, merit, or the effects of birth, alliance, or benefits, or with those accomplishments that support deference or obedience or respect.[9]

This natural equality is, of course, practically quite precarious, for powerful men may violate natural equity and exploit the weak. Since they do this "illegally" in nature, the victims remain free and equal "by right" even though not so in fact. Men always possess natural freedom and equality as a primary moral claim. By consent, they may establish unequal men, magistrates with special powers over them, but they do so in behalf of a more secure enjoyment of natural rights, and do not surrender the rights but only the prerogative of enforcement and punishment. They do that, said Althusius, in behalf of their own "prosperity and advantage," in order to have a "holy, just, comfortable, and happy" life. Any covenant to establish a government either assumes or specifically includes these ends. Morally, men cannot covenant away their natural rights, for they rest on God's authority.[10]

By 1600 natural-rights theory not only contained its full modern meaning but almost all of its distinctive vocabulary. Unlike ideas of popular sovereignty, it had no effective challenge until Hobbes. Even Bodin limited monarchical sovereignty by natural law. Machiavelli seemed to challenge the natural-law tradition. In fact, he skirted it. He pointed out, quite correctly, that natural-law theories provide no clear guide to politics and no suitable laws for the state. Natural law is too abstract, too much a body of lofty principles, to be of much practical use for a statesman. In an actual society, conflicting interests will lay claim to natural rights—the hungry will claim a natural right to food as readily as the rich will emphasize their natural right to property. The resolution of such conflict must be at the level of expediency and power. A civil society does not originate in a compact of moral philosophers but from the arts of often unscrupulous princes. Men accept authority and obey it, not because of its congruence with moral abstractions but out of self-interest, including fear of punishment. One who is trying to understand political behavior or to become a successful politician can gain little from natural-law theories except possibly appealing rationalizations. This line of argument, so identified with *The Prince*, did not mean that Machiavelli intellectually rejected the main Western moral tradition. He simply spoke of other issues and moved into a new universe of political discourse. He left moral philosophy for the more prosaic field of political science, and looked at the parameters of actual political behavior and speculated brilliantly on the *art* of political mastery.

Hobbes was different. He bearded the giant in its own den. Not only did he deny the practical utility of natural law but he also denied any juristic authority and any moral status to traditional natural-law doctrines. Hobbes realized that theories about natural law and right and resulting rationalizations of popular resistance to tyranny cohered with a vast body of Western philosophy and theology. In brief, they rested on some conception of an abstract moral order. Plato and Aristotle were the cultural devils, for they first advertised a belief in pure essence, in abstract rationality, in inherent purposes, or in a spurious kingdom of ideas. They passed their immaterialism, their demonology, on to the Western Church, which departed from the simple, concrete Jewish conception of a worldly kingdom and substituted the superstitious idea of the Church as a spiritual kingdom. Even when Protestants overthrew the Catholic church, or the Prince of Darkness, and rejected the spurious claims of pope and priests, they kept the Greek immaterialism, the allegiance to an elusive kingdom of reason and abstract right. To restore a proper Jewish view of man, of nationhood, and of religion, Hobbes attempted a revolution in Christian theology and then used his theological position to buttress an extreme form of political absolutism.

Hobbes would not speculate about the nature of God. But he was emphatic in his contention that the universe, God's creation, was in all ways a corporeal entity. All scriptural references to spirits, to mind or soul, reflected only a commonsense recognition of a difference between ponderable matter and aerial phenomena, such as wind or the "breath of life." No immaterialism was implied. Anticipating nineteenth-century adventists, Hobbes rejected a separable soul, any spiritual existence after death, any continuity of life between death and a future resurrection, and any unending torment for the damned (death or complete extinction in an eternal pit was their punishment). As he conceived it, the Kingdom of God was a real kingdom, presaged in the theocracy of the early Jews under Abraham and Moses. In the future, Jesus would return as sovereign over an earthly kingdom, inhabited by resurrected and bodily Christians living very much as they were then except no longer faced with death. Above all Hobbes wanted to refute the idea that the Church was the Kingdom of God. Hobbes believed the word *Church*, already a bundle of ambiguities, could best refer to a united body of Christians under a common jurisdiction or sovereignty. Thus, *the Church* is coterminous with a Christian commonwealth. Christians make up only an informal, nonjuristic body, not a church, in a non-Christian commonwealth.

In this perspective, *church* and *state* represent functional distinctions within one sovereign entity. The sovereign, as head of the church as well as the state, determines the scriptural canon, defines the correct public beliefs, decides what is heretical, establishes the public forms of worship, sanctions the sacraments, appoints all subordinate ecclesiastical officials, and has final powers of excommunication. The sovereign, in other words, assumes all the powers ever conceded to any pope or institutional church. Christian ministers only teach and counsel, without any juristic powers unless granted to them by the sovereign. Since the sovereign defines correct doctrines, by definition there can be no private right to teach or proclaim deviant beliefs. But Hobbes did recognize the autonomy of private conscience. Belief is not voluntary and not open to any type of governmental control. A dutiful Christian has to conform to all externals of the official religion, but believes as he must. God requires only faith (belief and love) and obedience. One can only meet the test of obedience by submitting to his sovereign in all areas, for obedience entails law and the only law now existent for man is the law of the state.

By denying abstract rationality, and any private right to determine moral obligations, Hobbes could define law in a positive way only. It is the will of a supreme power. Sovereignty, the absolute power to punish, makes right and wrong. It makes no sense to talk of a law without a coercive power ready to enforce it. God, in the past, established theocratic kingdoms and legislated for them. But the law given through Moses was real and concrete and strictly enforced. In Jesus, God prepared the way for a future kingdom, equally real and concrete. But until it comes, God left man subject to worldly power, to existing earthly sovereigns, who reign as God's agents on earth. Outwardly, and in all things, Jesus commanded Christians to obey this authority. Even if a king commands what seems to an individual to be a grievous sin, a Christian still must obey him as a Christian duty, leaving all responsibility to the sovereign and all punishment to God. A Christian cannot interject his own private interpretation of right and wrong. He should realize that his own salvation is never jeopardized by such obedience but only by rebellion against a sovereign. Here Hobbes clearly expressed his weariness of contentious religious debate. By someone's private judgment, almost any act of the sovereign will seem ungodly, and to allow resistance on the basis of private conscience seemed an invitation to anarchy.

Hobbes entered the lair of theologians to disarm the selfish and seditious appeals of papists and Puritans to the laws of God and of nature against the laws of the state. Despite the false teachings of popes, or priests, or dissenting ministers, God commands complete obedience to all earthly powers. Hobbes wanted to show that such obedience was more than a Christian responsibility, that it also reflected good moral science and good reason, that it rested on deductions from nature that were almost arithmetic in their compelling logic. Like most of his contemporaries, he believed the state was an artificial contrivance, created either by voluntary compact or by conquest, and highly desirable in either case. Men outside a commonwealth, outside the scope of coercive power and law, are equal, and free to do what they will short of limits set by physical law. For Hobbes, the equality entailed more than an absence of dependency. He believed human abilities varied but little, human passions hardly at all. In fact, throughout his political philosophy, Hobbes espoused a radical equalitarianism, although critics could always point out that it was not surprising that slaves were equal to each other. Whereas most everyone who appealed to a state of nature found in it the justification for a compact and some form of political authority (Locke charted its "inconveniences"), Hobbes painted the situation in the darkest possible colors. Men, in a state of nature, are literally at war with each other, and in large part because of their equality, because of the lack of any natural aristocracy, of any hierarchy of talents or righteousness. Most earlier accounts of the state of nature had assumed that some men, perhaps most men, most of the time, would perceive the long-run utility of natural law, and that in their best moments they would obey it and fairly enforce it within the limited sphere of their individual power. To Hobbes this assumption smacked of complete sophistry. It also revealed the false pretensions of elitists—of priests, or sorcerers, or philosopher kings who believed they had some special ability to perceive this vaporous natural law, but who in fact used natural-law sophistries to seduce the common people into sedition.

For Hobbes the first rule of reason for men in a state of nature was to get out of it as quickly as possible. They should transfer their natural but largely empty freedom to an artificial person, to the sovereign head of a commonwealth. They should do that in behalf of self-preservation, peace, order, security, and some chance of happiness. Instead of covenanting to enforce or preserve law, they covenant to *have* law. Instead of covenanting according to moral standards, they covenant to *have* a moral order. Once they create this artificial self, or in a sense pool their individual wills in one common will, they obviously have no private wills left and no recourse against the will of the sovereign. But sovereign power has natural limits. A king cannot overrule physics or monitor the private thoughts of individuals. Finally, Hobbes recognized a carefully circumscribed right of rebellion. One submits to an absolute sovereign in behalf of the order necessary to preserve life. By logic, one has no possible reason to obey a sovereign when one's own life or liberty (meaning only a freedom from impressment) is at stake. A prisoner, in a sense, is back in a state of nature and can do as he wills, which will undoubtedly mean attempts to escape.

Hobbes's case for absolutism was brilliant and revolutionary. He challenged the very heart of Christian orthodoxy in the West, and in England challenged a hallowed legal tradition. It was blasphemous to deny the reality of spirit and almost traitorous to deny any objective content to law. The accusation of atheism, absurd on the surface, well revealed the sheer horror of many people who read Hobbes's *Leviathan*. Yet, Hobbes immensely influenced subsequent political theory. His mode of analysis and concern for concreteness set a standard for later philosophers. Hobbes had little influence on English politics and almost no disciples in England or in America. Even the defenders of royal absolutism could follow the orthodox Filmer and retain a belief in natural law, as most did. It never seemed necessary to destroy the whole Western philosophic tradition in order to oppose rebellion and sedition. But since natural-law theories retained such a broad appeal in the eighteenth century, and so much conditioned American justifications of a revolution,

Hobbes provided, by sheer contrast, and by the most incisive
challenge possible, the best insight into what these theories really meant, and into their strengths and weaknesses.[11]

In a practical sense, Hobbes added to the many political
claims addressed to the English people in a time of civil war. He
tried to persuade his audience that both self-interest and piety
dictated complete obedience to the existing British monarch.
The generality of his theories hardly disguised his favoritism for
absolute monarchy, his clever appeals to popular opinion, and
his frequent offers of practical advice to kings. In his way,
Hobbes addressed a moral appeal to the people. By compelling
logic, not sovereign edict, he tried to persuade people that it was
"right" to obey a sovereign in all circumstances, and thus himself appealed to a category of right and of compelling law that
existed only in a realm of discourse or, in his own derogatory
terms, in a realm of words or mere opinion. Conceived in this
way, his words competed with opposite words—it is not "right"
to obey a prince under all circumstances, to surrender to a unified will all responsibility for determining what is "right" and
"wrong." Hobbes knew that, physically, men could and often
did rebel, and in some cases successfully. When that occurred
he clearly lost his battle of words and could only cry out his futile imprecations against fools. For not only in England, but
then in America and in France, Sidney and Locke won the verbal conflict, and in the process proved the immense practical import of "mere" theories about moral good.

Algernon Sidney, who wrote the most detailed refutation of
Filmer, directed many of his arguments at Hobbes. He added
nothing new to natural-law theories, but spoke with convincing
passion and occasional eloquence. Appealing to a legal tradition
that stretched back to Bracton, he insisted that a legitimate king
gained all his power from law and ultimately from God. A king
who ruled arbitrarily, against natural justice and against property, was not an agent of God but of Satan, for no unjust
power could derive from God. But as Hobbes pointed out, God
did not govern in England and did not enforce any special set of

laws there. What meaning could one give to a "higher law" from God when no sovereign power defined and enforced it? How could anyone arbitrate among the contending private interpretations of this alleged law?

Sidney tried to answer these questions. He could easily assert the old orthodoxy, that God's law was in the form of a "universal reason, to which all nations, at all times, owe an equal veneration and obedience." But are its terms self-evident, beyond honest dispute? At times Sidney skirted this challenge with a typical British response. He appealed to "ancient inherent liberties," to the existing English legal system, as if it somehow contained all of natural right. If there remained an uncertainty about natural law, then he appealed to the legislative and juristic role of Parliament, to a representative body which spoke for the people, who in some sense had to be the final arbiters of "lawfulness." Presumably, Parliament would adhere to the spirit of the past and always abide by a law "above all passion, void of desire and fear, lust and anger," to an "ultimate reason, retaining some measure of divine perfection," with no regard for person; commanding the good, punishing the evil; deaf, inexorable, inflexible. All men know it, and under it are "governed by God, rather than by men. . . ." [12]

But Sidney could not rest his case on English tradition or the wisdom of Parliament. In some sense, the overarching principles of natural law had to be crystal clear to all sane or right-minded men. Here Sidney's logic was old, but also as current as Allied justifications of the Nuremberg trials. Surely, he reasoned, a basic conception of right is rooted in common sense, in conscience, in our very nature. He suggested that certain legal axioms were as obvious as Euclidian geometry. [13] In more modern language, he suggested that men could make certain sure inferences from some necessary, and thus universal, aspects of any organized society. The state of nature, either as a viable possibility or only an analytical tool, helped clarify Sidney's claim. In a state of nature men are equally free because they are equally nondependent. By consent they give up this equality and establish a government, but only for rational and self-justifying reasons, for such utilitarian goals as security for life and property. These goals indicate the broad limits of justice and establish beyond doubt the extremes of injustice. It is obvious that one should not arbitrarily take a life, enslave another man, or, much the same thing, steal all the products of his labor. Simple, logical consistency justifies the obvious. To use later, Kantian language, a sane man simply cannot sanction murder, slavery, and robbery as universal rules of conduct, for to do so would be to affirm his own suffering and early death, since no man is omnipotent, powerful enough to be on the winning side in every brutal conflict with all other men. In this sense, these natural rights, although elusive in detail and in their exact implication in varying contexts, are simply aspects of self-affirmation, of one's continuous insistence upon a degree of integrity and worth. They are inherent in the human condition, present wherever aspiring man is present, and in no sense a gift of artificial sovereigns, although sovereign power may be a necessary tool to ensure the actual enjoyment of such rights.

Hobbes and Sidney were indeed far apart, but their arguments rarely clashed as brutally as Sidney assumed. Semantic traps concealed the nature of the gulf. Hobbes said might makes right, which is undeniable if *right* means an operative privilege that one can actually exercise. Sidney said right gives legitimacy to power. This claim is undeniable if *legitimacy* denotes a psychological stance toward power, a willing complaisance, a feeling of rightness, a balm of conscience. Hobbes used *law* to mean concrete commands. Sidney used it to designate the object of felt obligation, or for what Hobbes contemptuously called mere words. Sidney remained a moral philosopher, exploring the dimensions of certain of his own preferences that seemed so inseparably connected to his humanity that all men surely shared them. Thus, he could move from an asserted but loosely specified esthetic to a political ethic that seemed to become moral man, that harmonized with an idealized conception of man, as well as provided motives for courageous political commitment or

NATURAL RIGHTS / 94

even, for Sidney, political martyrdom. Hobbes remained a political scientist, possibly the greatest of all time. He was always
careful to restrict his analysis to the hard realities of power and
to define law and right in this operational context. What made
him unique was not his deliberate eschewal of moral abstractions (Machiavelli anticipated him here), but his determination
to squeeze all the traditional language and meaning of moral philosophy into his political science. Heretofore Western moralists
had too often failed to note the proper distinction between normative and descriptive theory, between moral law and positive
law, or they had allowed the moral to swallow up the positive.
Hobbes reversed the odds. Instead of properly distinguishing
two autonomous realms of discourse, he tried vainly to absorb
the moral into the descriptive, and thus denied any validity to
the old paths of moral philosophy.

In most ways John Locke only composed a beautifully concise, lofty, impersonal summary of the natural-law tradition. As
a professional philosopher he easily transcended the contextual
urgencies and the personal involvements of Sidney. Even
Hobbes never communicated the same sense of detached wisdom, of persuasive reasonableness, of almost axiomatic assurance. Locke spoke with the assurance of a long tradition, and
rightfully castigated the modernity of Hobbes and Filmer, or
new-fangled doctrines of absolutism scarcely a hundred years
old. Locke also recognized the moral context of all natural-law
theories. Such theories of law instruct men in their duties and
obligations, help individuals make correct moral choices that
have immense practical and psychological consequences. More
than most of his predecessors, Locke appealed directly to self-interest, to the utilitarian side of natural rights. In a moral universe, law is not a restraint on human action so much as a guide,
a clarified sense of direction, for "free and intelligent" agents, for
men who seek their proper interests and the general good. Such
a moral law justifies itself by its consequences. It guides man
toward happiness and prevents misery. It preserves and enlarges
his freedom, his possibilities of self-fulfillment. It shows a way

to organize a society in order to prevent subjection to the arbitrary will of others.[14]

From Locke's strictly moral perspective, man always has his natural rights. Men who join in a political society do not surrender rights (such inherent moral attributes are not alienable by definition), but do give up to a government their former individual prerogative of enforcing natural law. They do so in the happy expectation that their rights will be more secure, more realizable, in a context of public law. Men compact in vain if government ceases to be a protector and becomes the new oppressor. At that point those who govern lose all power rooted in trust, and use only the power rooted in sheer strength. They literally wage war on the people. All moral obligation, based as it is on the now subverted purposes of government, ceases, and the community resumes all the rights of enforcement surrendered to a formerly legitimate government. The moral duty of citizens remains the upholding of law and justice, but now they correctly uphold law by enforcing it upon governmental oppressors. Since they resist tyranny in behalf of law and moral order they are in no sense rebels. The oppressive government alone is guilty of rebellion and treason.

In a tantalizingly brief but immensely significant discussion, Locke added new subtleties to an often asserted right of property. He contributed more at the level of careful distinctions than at the level of belief. He, in effect, articulated the full implications of the Calvinist doctrine of a calling and a derivative labor theory of value. Long before he wrote, the English Puritans had espoused similar doctrines and in New England even implemented them in their institutions. In a more general way, Locke fitted traditional Christian views of responsible ownership to new economic realities.

To refute Filmer's ascription of all propriety to Adam and his monarchical successors, Locke contended that a carefully qualified form of property was a natural right, inherent in the very conditions under which man occupies God's world. Locke used the word *property* loosely, often expanding it to encompass all natural rights, beginning with one's property in oneself and in one's own labor. Locke concurred with many of his medieval predecessors: God did give the earth to man in common. By right the earth remained a common possession so long as men simply gathered its fruits (as did Indians in parts of America). But by the labor of the gathering a person extended himself into the fruit, assimilated it to his own personality, and thus made it his own. In exchange, its legitimate value was only the labor expended in the gathering and not any value added by scarcity, for man has no natural or inherent moral right to capitalize an unearned increment. Even the right of possession through labor has limits, for one cannot rightfully possess more perishable fruits than he needs for his own use, and has a moral obligation to share any surplus with neighbors in need.

The most basic form of property is not consumable goods but enclosed parts of the earth, or access to the primary source of all sustenance. That God gave the earth to man in common entailed, to Locke, one moral stipulation: no one can monopolize nature or permanently exclude others from access to it. The right to property, at its most critical level, remains the right to share in nature and, in a developed society which requires cultivation, the right to have access to productive land or other natural resources. It is a positive right of access and not just the privilege of retaining what one has. Locke believed labor expended in the development and improvement of nature, or by implication any capital formation by a producer (emphatically not by an investor), gave one the same right of exclusive use as does labor expended in the gathering of fruit. He thus defined assured access to enclosed fields, exclusive, individual management of that land or other comparable means of production, and a full enjoyment of the resultant production as natural rights, essential to the fullest development of personality and to all prospects of realized happiness.

But because Locke generalized such property into a right of nature, universally applicable, he had to qualify it very carefully. One can as a natural right only enclose the part of nature actually needed; one cannot own any part that he does not use, cannot accumulate any surplus of land or its consumable products, and, most restrictive, cannot possess it at all unless other land, of equal quality, remains available for others. His natural property does not require any single system of tenure, but does require some secure access rights for individuals and the right of inheritance. The father has a right to labor in behalf of his children, and they have a right to gain a vested right in land through their own filial labor. If a person's alleged property meets all these criteria, then to Locke it is as sacred as life itself and almost inseparable from life. No one, and no government, can rightly take any or all of this natural property without the owner's express consent. This proviso gave the highest possible sanction to a traditional English principle: in the case of taxation, some form of representative assembly is morally necessary. No people can rightfully surrender to a prince any arbitrary powers over taxation. By this argument, and in this one area, natural-rights theory first suggested some form of electoral privilege. In a carefully circumscribed area, the right to vote may become a natural right.

Locke's natural property, as he realized, was not at all equivalent to many existing forms of property in England and other modern nations. Like other themes in natural law, his conception of natural property provided not a model of property law but a critical perspective for judging existing property regulations. Locke did not draw the practical implications, leaving room for quite divergent later interpretations, from avowed "capitalists" to Marxists to single taxers. His natural property most clearly precluded monopolies, or the involuntary exclusion of people from nature, leaving open the subtleties involved in the word *involuntary*. Locke clearly expected many peoople, by choice, to labor for others. It was also clear that no one could claim the sanction of nature for usury, for patent and copyright privileges, for unearned increments or scarcity values of any sort, for privileged access by franchise or corporate charter, or for any monetary wealth. Locke clearly gave the sanction of nature to a homestead gained and improved by labor, to the freedom needed to manage it or other comparable types of real property, and to the immediate products of one's labor. Governmental regulations in these areas had to apply to means, not to substance, and are best illustrated by laws governing titles to land. More radical in later implications, the natural right to property seemed to give to unpropertied men, with no realizable access to a part of nature, a moral right to expropriate any excess or surplus land or goods held by another, even if held according to the positive law of a state.

To deduce the implications of Locke's natural property only is to distort the full thrust of his theory. He was part of a commercial society, and neither an atavistic foe of modernity nor an early socialist. By his analysis he had to deny any natural, objective, universal status to speculative property or to large accumulations of property. Later, after the development of corporate forms of property that he hardly anticipated, Locke's labor theory of value provided a strong moral weapon for Marxists. But as a matter of desirable public policy, Locke supported nonnatural forms of property so long as they did not deny or foreclose natural property rights. The leeway here seemed quite wide. Locke pointed out that, through consent, people agree to respect many forms of possession that do not meet the qualifications of natural law. Such property rests on positive law. Here Locke was not far from Hobbes. Whatever a sovereign legislature commands is the law. In the case of gold and silver, scarce nonconsumable objects useful as mediums of exchange, Locke seemed to believe that the consent was already universal, at least among civilized countries. Here was a valid form of conventional property, by its very nature not subject to natural limits on accumulation. Coined gold is not an item of sustenance, and even a monopoly of it would not, by itself, exclude anyone from subsistence. Only if used to control access to land or food does it become unlawful according to natural law. This example of money, the only form of conventional property that Locke analyzed, reveals the leeway open to a state in legalizing forms of property that do not conflict with natural rights. The type and the extent of such protected conventional property is simply an option open to legislators. Thus, Locke would have agreed with medieval churchmen that usury was not a natural form of property, but at the same time would have voted to make it a form of conventional and protected property in England. The same could be said for a wide variety of commercial paper, of bonds and even common stock.[15]

For Locke, as for most Americans even in the eighteenth century, the archetypal form of property was land. It not only made livelihood possible but also invited the most fulfilling forms of self-expression in its management. If man was to attain happiness, he had to find a large share of that happiness in his calling, in his daily work. The prime justification of the state was its necessity to provide security in property and in its management. The prime threat of slavery lay in a denial of property rights to all men. Locke recognized other hazards, believed in other expressive freedoms. He was a noted champion of religious toleration (not, be it noted, of separation of church and state) and, with Milton, a champion of freedom in speech and expanded areas of freedom in print (but in no sense an advocate of unrestricted freedom in the contemporary sense). At that time the traditional meaning of natural rights did not include complete religious liberty or completely unrestricted freedom of speech, press, and assembly. Perhaps, on careful analysis, these rights were deductive implications of life, liberty, and property in many social contexts, but only slowly did men make such deductions. It is ironic that today people often associate these expressive freedoms almost alone with natural rights.

Natural-rights theories climaxed in the eighteenth century. The proven utility of mechanical reasoning, the almost unlimited prospects for scientific inquiry, and the widespread hopes for a developed social science all supported the universalism and objectivism of natural-law reasoning. Even the growing emphasis upon a rationalized Christianity and the easy acceptance of God's benevolence reinforced doctrines of natural law, and helped shift the emphasis away from what God commanded to the means He provided for human happiness. Three eighteenth-century jurists, all celebrated in America, wrote learned treatises on natural law, applying its principles to both national and international law. One, Enrich de Vattel, emphasized that becoming a citizen of a state in no way released one from the unamendable principles of right reason, from one's obligation to do justice. He accepted Locke's qualified definition of natural property, and for the first time tried to apply natural-law principles to international trade and communication. Vattel saw certain unique implications for natural law in a pluralistic society. There, competing sects and factions have to have wide degrees of toleration and more expressive freedoms or they face a form of slavery. Natural justice often requires either toleration or new national divisions along ideological lines. The same requirements apply to separate colonies or provinces, a distinction with obvious implications for America.[16]

Baron Samuel Pufendorf, a Prussian, a staunch Lutheran, and the mentor of John Wise and other Americans in the eighteenth century, wrote a long tedious treatise on moral philosophy. In it he tried to prove the certainty of moral science and the deductive status of moral law. A critic of Hobbes, he argued that knowledge of what is upright and what is base is as secure as any other kind of knowledge. Laws founded in the very condition of man are not unclear or weak. The principles are certain, even though circumstances condition their application, a recognition of contextual relativity that had long been inherent but too often ignored by natural-law theorists. God does sanction property, or some access to nature and its goods, but He does not sanction any one system of tenure.[17]

Jean Jacques Burlamaqui, a professor at the University of Geneva, sought the same goals—a developed moral science and a deductive natural law. But much more than Pufendorf he made concessions to Hobbes. The end of man is happiness, and thus any moral theory must depart from self-love and a desire for self-preservation. Right is whatever reason certainly acknowledges as a full means of attaining happiness. In order to define those means, Burlamaqui made elaborate distinctions. He defined law, as had Hobbes, as the published will of a sovereign, but believed such laws gained legitimacy as internally felt obligations only when conformable to reason. Power commands action but not respect. Power without right cannot elicit the voluntary submission that is a necessary part of our happiness. He wanted a government with all the power of enforcement necessary to sustain law, yet wise and rational enough to issue the commands that would meet broad acceptance from reasonable men. In this way he tried to join the concrete, operative view of Hobbes with conventional Western conceptions of moral law.[18]

Scholarly jurists such as Pufendorf and Burlamaqui added special authority to later, American appeals to natural law. But the special heritage of law in America was always English. Sidney and Locke were the acknowledged prophets. The exact language, the flavor of argument, often the very phrases used by Americans, came either from eighteenth-century English polemicists and reformers or from native invention. The latter should not be minimized. But as Bernard Bailyn has so copiously documented, neither should the direct links to English dissenters and radicals fighting their own battles against the English establishment, crying out in unison with Americans their own jeremiads about British corruption and decay. They, like their American cousins, easily expanded the implications of natural rights to encompass almost any grievance or sense of injustice, often blending natural rights with obviously indigenous English traditions. But the sum of the indictment, on both sides, and as it has always been in political conflict, was a thunderous accusation—the British government treated its constituents unjustly and violated standards of right that men everywhere recognized and respected. The "decent opinion of mankind" required Americans to itemize these wrongs and show their relationship to universal moral principles.[19]

5. *In a Revolutionary*
Context

BEGINNING WITH THE STAMP ACT CRISIS, Americans continuously appealed to familiar natural rights. On the winning side "patriots" used the appeal in a vain effort to reverse
despised British policies. On the losing side "loyalists" used it in
vain attempts to protect their honor and their property, if not
their lives, against either mobs or discriminatory new laws
passed by state legislatures. The appeal to natural right was in
no way surprising and in all ways consistent with the dominant
moral theories of the day. Those who felt themselves suffering
under grave injustices simply wanted to prove that their grievances were not at a purely practical level, not just a matter of
simple policy or conflicting preferences, but that their persecu-
tors had violated universal and objective standards of right.

As the struggle with Britain developed, appeals to natural
rights served varying needs. From the Stamp Act crisis until the
Intolerable Acts, unhappy colonists continually condemned the
grave inequities of British policies and stressed the vulnerability
of their rights. Their appeal to fundamental rights quickly sur-
passed in volume, if not in effectiveness, practical appeals to
British self-interest. But except for a fervent minority the colonial leaders did not, in these years, deny their continued partici-

pation in the larger British nation or claim any complete exemption from parliamentary authority. Instead, they sought relief within the system, including more local autonomy and local control over taxes. In a sovereign community an appeal to natural rights justifies internal changes, such as the deposition of an unjust government, but only as a desperate last resort can it vindicate the fragmentation of a country into several sovereign entities.

The colonial claim of local sovereignty changed the bearing of natural-rights arguments. After 1774 the advanced colonial appeal was to colonial legislative autonomy under a common monarch. In the American view, this local autonomy dated back to settlement and rested on the natural right of emigration and of forming original compacts. The colonies paralleled opening hostilities against Britain with futile appeals to their king to uphold their rights. Then, in 1776, they declared their independence, not from Parliament (by their developed theory they had never been subject to Parliament) but from the person of the king. At this point they used natural-rights theory to justify the overthrow of a tyrannical monarch and the substitution of new, republican forms of government.

The appeal to natural rights was an obvious strategy to anyone in the Christian West who wanted to protest felt injustices. Particularly in New England, the libertarian heritage of early Calvinists and the precedents of the English revolutions remained a vital part of a revered heritage. Next to the Bible, Locke was the greatest authority for politically concerned ministers. In almost all colonies internal clashes between competing economic interests, or unending conflicts between assemblies and royal governors, had kept alive a tradition of polemics and appeals to grandiose principles. Just as important, Americans enjoyed, *de facto*, an unusual degree of expressive freedom. As the struggle developed, and wherever opinion favored the colonial side, the patriots spoke and printed freely, almost arrogantly. Nor even in the exaggerated litany of abuse in the Declaration of Independence could they accuse Britain of any effective repression of speech, press, or assembly. In fact, the patriots were in almost all cases the effective suppressors and the loyalists the suppressed. In this atmosphere of freedom, colonial advocates first marshalled their arguments to counter not severe inroads of tyranny but a small tax, which, as they viewed it, threatened much worse to come.

The moral theory behind the colonial appeals was familiar to most literate Americans and a commonplace of New England pulpits. In a 1762 election sermon before the Massachusetts General Court, the Reverend Abraham Williams gave an unusually concise and eloquent statement of natural rights and a moral conception of the state. Following Locke very closely, Williams emphasized an original natural equality, the several inconveniences attendant to a state of nature made up of sometimes errant and sinful men, and the logic of covenants to establish limited governments. As much as his Puritan progenitors, Williams emphasized that government authority came mediately from man but ultimately from God. Thus, government was "a divine Constitution, founded in the Nature and Relations of Things." Its end "must be to secure the Rights and Properties of its Members, and promote their Welfare . . ."; in order that they may possess the proper rewards of "honest industry" and enjoy all "the Conveniencies of a social Life, to which Uprightness entitles them . . . ," and that the "Unjust and rapacious" be restrained and the ill effects of their wickedness prevented. Men surrender to government only the right they formerly had of executing righteous judgments. It is therefore the duty of a government to defend its citizens, to secure their property from foreign invasion, to preserve order and peace, and to execute justice among its members.[1]

Williams found his guidelines for attaining those ends in a law of nature to which all men are subject (in 1750 another minister, Jonathan Mayhew, even alleged that God himself was subject to it). In a state of nature each man has God's authority to enforce natural law and to seek redress for its violations. In an organized society, government takes over this responsibility and fulfills it through published, equitable laws sufficient to secure rights and property. But, as Williams emphasized, these civil laws "are, or ever ought to be, only the Laws of Nature explained and applied, both Laws and Sanctions being founded in Reason and Equity." Content with the existing church establishment in Massachusetts, he still stressed that the human mind is beyond the control of law and that religious belief must be free. The right of conscience is unalienable and inseparable from our nature. In its most vital respect, religion is internal and personal. Yet, any good society will encourage and support public worship and institutions conducive to righteousness.[2]

The Stamp Act moved ideas of natural rights from the pulpit to the marketplace. For protesting Americans the Stamp Act and later Townshend duties seemed not only unwise but immoral and illegal. Property, at least in one's estate and in the products of one's own labor, was a natural right and subject to no government duties without explicit consent. Thus, only directly representative colonial assemblies had any right to tax Americans. This argument won broad assent in America and secured a broader agreement in England than any subsequent colonial position. Cautious moderates like Daniel Dulaney of Maryland, who stressed the lack of representation in Parliament of American property owners as a distinct class, joined flaming radicals, such as the author of *The Constitutional Courant*, who defined the Stamp Act as a form of slavery and saw it as evidence that Parliament had declared war on all the rights of American Englishmen. According to him, a slave was one who depended on the will of another for the enjoyment of life and property. Deprivation of a part of one's estate might, in time, lead to the deprivation of the whole and even of life itself. One Puritan clergyman, Stephen Johnson of Lyme, Connecticut, even argued that the Stamp Act, alone, annulled the Connecticut charter and dissolved all connection with Britain. The people were back in a state of nature, ripe for a new covenant.[3]

For strategic reasons, the appeal to natural rights, although widely present even in 1765, almost always took second place to appeals to charter rights or to the rights under the "British Constitution." The same right was at stake in each case—property, although rarely a clearly defined form of property. Property was not only a natural right but also a right long recognized in British law. In one sense of the ambiguous word, it was a "constitutional" right. Since many colonial charters granted to Americans all the rights of Englishmen, it was also a charter right. But among the three levels of status, charters and constitutions did not have the same explosive potential, the same revolutionary appeal, as nature or God. When New England clergymen used natural rights as an excuse for the annulment of a charter and a return to a state of nature, one can understand why moderates even in the First Continental Congress preferred to base their petitions on the legally established, constitutional rights of British citizens.

The Stamp Act Congress stressed the constitutional issues. Americans had all the essential freedoms of natural-born subjects, including the right of consent in taxation. Only in a special address to the king did the congress refer to "inherent rights and liberties." Most colonial partisans, sooner or later, used such words as *inherent, natural,* or *God-given* to suggest the ultimate source of their rights. James Otis, as early as 1764, cleverly touched all bases, affirming that "by the law of God and nature," as well as by common law and act of Parliament, Americans were entitled to all "the natural, essential, inherent and inseparable rights of our fellow subjects in Great Britain. . . ." John Adams, in his earliest contribution to the political controversy, drew the exact relationship between British and natural rights. British liberties, he said, "are not the grants of princes or parliaments but original rights, conditions of original contracts, coequal with prerogative and coeval with government." Many of these rights "are inherent and essential, agreed on as maxims and established as preliminaries even before a parliament existed." Thus, he suggested that the ultimate place to search for the foundations of British laws was in "human nature, in the constitution of the intellectual and moral world." [4]

Few writers made as detailed an analysis as Adams. Some moderates, such as Joseph Galloway and John Dickinson, rarely if ever appealed to God or nature, resting their case on property rights acknowledged in England. New Englanders had a greater penchant for ultimate sources of law. Samuel Adams almost always clinched his arguments with appeals to nature, even as he clarified his position with references to the state of nature. Human rights, he asserted in 1772, derive from the duty of self-preservation, remain with the individual when he enters an organized society, and limit all legitimate positive law to what is reasonable and equitable, for the very end of civil government is the "support, protection and defense of . . . life, liberty, and property." In 1773, in a letter to other colonies, the Massachusetts House bemoaned the abridgement of English liberties by Parliament, and then attributed these rights to "the laws of nature, and the English constitution." As early as 1765 the Virginia House of Burgesses, never willing to be outdone in its fervor by the Puritans of Massachusetts, stressed that Parliament was limited by its own constitution and by the "original inherent rights" of citizens.[5]

Only John Adams suggested any valid distinctions to be drawn between natural and British rights. As in the past, few Americans stopped to distinguish between the grand ends of government and the contextually determined means to those ends. One could appeal to nature in behalf of life or certain carefully qualified forms of property. One could appeal to a wide range of procedural guarantees in the common law when under indictment for a criminal offense. These procedures rested, not on any deduction from nature or from the universal situation of man, but on an implied, unwritten covenant among Englishmen. The colonial apprehension over suspension of jury trials in the enforcement of the Stamp Act related to British rights and not natural rights, to covenant and good faith and not God's edict. But it was simpler to blend or merge all forms of right and to make the most expedient appeal in any situation. That Americans did.

The crucial point of contention, the springboard of all subsequent controversy, was taxation. Here the colonists could appeal with equal ease to British tradition and conventional theories of natural law. Not that taxation by Parliament was an illegitimate legislative function. Legislatures must tax if any governmental body has the power of raising revenue. But since taxes involve private property they require consent. Few Englishmen could disagree on this. No natural-law argument could necessitate popular participation except in this one vital area. But parliamentary usurpation here would surely lead, said apprehensive colonists, to other forms of suppression that were, inherently, arbitrary and contrary to law. Since the American insistence on consent was irrefutable on principle, the British had to shift the controversy to the prosaic problem of representation. Perhaps their insistence on vicarious representation made sense in England, where examples of absurd underrepresentation, at least on a geographical basis, abounded, but the same arguments seemed devious and hypocritical to Americans, since here almost all owners of real property had the vote and some sense of participation in tax legislation.

The logic of the American position, short of colonists' later appeal to colonial sovereignty, did not of necessity lead to the American goal of local legislative autonomy on all revenue bills. It could have provoked a disarming (and, to many revolutionaries, a crushing) British response—American representatives in Parliament with, at the very minimum, a voice and vote on all tax measures affecting the colonies. Nothing in natural-law theory required any broader popular representation in government. Natural law required only a moral outcome from government, however elected or appointed. There is no necessity, perhaps no clear likelihood, that elective and responsive governments are uniquely solicitous of life, liberty, and property, particularly for despised minorities. But any government requires funds in order to operate. How secure them? Medieval kings often relied upon their own, personal properties. Otherwise they had to beg funds from private citizens, or else take it from them by some form of coercion. The need, joined with the obvious possibilities of abuse, led to the unique English accommodation. The people had the right to acquiesce in all grants. The English House of Commons began as an assemblage of propertied knights, or selected representatives, who met to approve special grants to the king. From this heritage developed the English and American tradition that money bills should originate in the lower house. The same concern led, in all the colonies, to suffrage rights for freeholders, just as it reinforced traditional franchise restrictions against those without real property.

Since Americans continually appealed to life, liberty, and above all to property, what precisely did they mean by these words? In many ways, *life* was the neglected term in the trilogy. Had Britain tried to impress Americans into armies or executed swift justice by firing squads, then appeals to the right of self-preservation might have figured more often in the verbal controversies. John Adams often stressed the rule of law as the key to a secure life, and any type of private revenge or vigilante justice as a continuing threat to life. Without laws and fair enforcement one could be killed at any moment. Often in 1775 and 1776 extralegal colonial assemblies justified their governmental role by the very absence of any British authority, by a forfeiture of authority by those who had formerly ruled and who, ironically, often fled as a result of colonial mobs. In this sense the right of life implied a right to have a protective government, to have laws and courts, and suggested the procedural safeguards of the common law that helped preclude the conviction and execution of innocent people. It also suggested the dangers of martial law or a military dictatorship, and thus the suspension of such safeguards. But the issues most often at stake with Britain involved the quality of life and not its continuance, the possibilities of happiness and not the prospects of early death.

Liberty and property were the most embracing concerns but scarcely separate concerns. Property rights—ownership, management, returns—alone could assure one liberty. In the tradition of natural rights, liberty still meant autonomy or nondependence. Over and over again Americans indicted British policies as steps toward slavery or, in their most fervent exaggerations, as the very substance of slavery. No single word better expressed their fear. Possibly, as John Burke suggested, it came easily to mind and carried intense meaning because Americans knew slavery firsthand. Long accustomed to near autonomy, happy to collect the diplomatic and economic benefits of British citizenship, and long able to minimize the costs of such dependency, colonial leaders could easily interpret the Stamp Act as an awful omen of the future. If, in principle, a distant Britain could tax the colonies at will, then America was already an inferior dependency and Americans were already in some sense slaves, without full control over their own destiny. Viewed from this perspective, the reasonableness of British taxes was not important. A well-treated slave remains a slave, always subject to his master's will. The right of self-taxation symbolized equality with home Englishmen, while British claims of unlimited powers of taxation symbolized dependency. Too often it seemed as if superior addressed inferior and in a much more threatening way than in the recent past.

American Negro slavery embarrassed the American appeals to liberty. Contrary to later interpretations, wide extremes of wealth, clear class differences, forms of deference, even temporary and voluntary servitude or employment were all consistent with natural freedom and equality. Involuntary servitude for life for innocent people was emphatically not consistent. Americans could not deny the logic of Samuel Hopkins, a Calvinist minister and protegé of Jonathan Edwards and an early harbinger of later abolitionists. In the vital year of 1776 he noted that the suffering of Negro slaves exceeded by a hundredfold the sufferings of the Sons of Liberty, and incorrectly prophesised that Americans would not win victory before emancipation. Jefferson, in his "Summary View of the Rights of British America," and in an early draft of the Declaration of Independence, tried to place all the blame for slavery upon Britain. In his view the colonists had tried to stop the awful slave trade but the king vetoed their efforts, and so the "right of human nature" had been "deeply wounded by this infamous practice." His argument was disingenuous at best.[6]

The various arguments for Negro slavery did not touch the issue of natural rights. The alleged racial inferiority of Negroes, for example, could not excuse slavery. From the perspective of natural rights, extreme inequalities of ability did not justify one person's controlling the destiny of another, for in nature all are equally free and only consent can legitimatize any form of rule even by the able over the less capable. Negroes, however inferior they seemed, were still human and thus heirs to all natural rights. They might volunteer service for a specified time period, as did white servants, but they did not even have the right to alienate their own freedom permanently, much less that of their children. Jefferson deeply felt the dilemma. He was often ambivalent in his views of the Negro race, but never in his condemnation of human slavery. His abstract theories about man and about human origins suggested the rough equality of varied human races, provided one could develop clear criteria for establishing equality. But his direct observations on his and neighboring plantations led him to a much more harsh estimate of Negro capabilities. He never had a final answer on this issue but he did realize that it was not pertinent to the moral issue. Later, those such as Calhoun who offered an elaborate vindication of Negro slavery had to begin by challenging the whole theory of natural rights.

Property was the most obvious issue in 1776. On this point there was little controversy. Life and liberty depend on access to nature, on the autonomy that property allows, on the right to enjoy the fruits of one's own labors. John Hancock said it more forcefully than anyone else; security to person and property (he did not separate the two) "is so obviously the design and end of civil government, that to attempt a logical proof of it, would be like burning tapers at noonday, to assist the sun in enlightening the world. . . ." A nonconsentful taking of property, taxation without representation, was the most focused charge against Britain. Yet, there were ambiguities in the colonial appeals to property.[7]

In 1776 the word *property* suggested, above all else, farmland. In many contexts people talked about their "estates" rather than their "possessions." This agricultural image was natural in a country in which ninety percent of the people earned their livelihood from farming. Few were the men who engaged in commercial undertakings or in the professions without also owning land and at least supervising agricultural enterprises. In the South, in particular, many large planters were also merchants and on occasion also lawyers. But other images attached to the word *property*. At times it encompassed even slaves as well as land as a speculative commodity, rather than a homestead or the means of production. A few reformers, a few New England ministers, at times an idealistic Jefferson still used *property* in the restrictive, natural sense idealized by Locke. But few Americans made such narrow distinctions. In its ideal sense, and the only sense at all related to natural rights, property included access to a part of nature needed for sustenance and used productively, as well as to the resultant products of one's labor. This property did not preclude the comforts and conveniences of a gentleman but rather, as Locke made clear, justified these attainments. But it did not include slaves, speculative holdings, or the vehicles of commerce (the "paper and patronage" of John Taylor).

Jefferson eventually acknowledged that many legally recognized forms of property in America had no natural status and thus rested only on popular consent. They were creatures of legislative or constitutional process and, unlike natural rights, always subject to such process. The ambiguities of meaning in the word *property* invited a moral inversion—the use of natural-law concepts to spread a veil of sanctity around all forms of possessions or wealth, a moral travesty best revealed in Southern efforts to protect property in slaves. Happily, Jefferson's substitution of "pursuit of happiness" for property in the Declaration of Independence bypassed these ambiguities. Happiness had long occupied a dominant position in the rhetoric of natural rights. By general consent it was the prime end of government, even as some form of property, some protected access to nature and its products, was a necessity for happiness. In 1776 either "pursuit of happiness" or "equality of opportunity" best expressed the moral content of Locke's "natural property." The word *property* already stood for too many nonnatural possessions and anchored too many politically vested privileges. The ambiguities, as usual, created an opportunity for hypocrisy. Jefferson was in a minority in seeking means to make natural property a positive guarantee for all Americans. He vainly sought a fifty-acre birthright for all Virginians, and lamented huge, speculative estates accumulated largely through political favoritism. In the end he won only a minor skirmish by the abolition of primogeniture and entail, but hoped the Louisiana purchase would insure open lands into a distant future and that all Americans would have the opportunity to be free—that is, to own property.

As a propaganda appeal, property was wonderful. Except for Negroes, most American family heads owned, or confidently expected to own, some real property. Condemnation of British threats to property helped mute conflicts between large and small property owners, helped disguise the very different status of farmland and investment property, and postponed the almost inevitable conflict between agricultural and commercial interests. During the Revolution, and particularly in the federal convention of 1787, the owners or proponents of commercial property exerted an influence all out of proportion to their numbers, and worked assiduously and in the main successfully to secure and expand the security of such instruments of commerce as a sound and stable currency, a national banking system, and protected contracts, franchises, and corporate charters. In some cases conventional forms of property, such as protected holdings in speculative lands, bestowed vast social increments on a few daring or politically favored men, which in turn increased the cost of land for homesteaders. In this sense, some forms of legally recognized property were inherently monopolistic and already threatened the forms of property that qualified as natural rights.

Perhaps the talk of happiness, so endemic in the natural-law tradition, begged the most critical issue. What, specifically, constitutes happiness? Is it really obvious or the same for all people? Possibly our eighteenth-century progenitors sought the public means for an unclear or undefined goal. And, indeed, their emphasis was continuously upon means, upon political instruments. They assumed and celebrated rather vague goals. Franklin, in his impatience with ethical disputation, with all abstract discussions of man's highest end, often seemed to assume no great difficulties in ends—surely all virtuous men know the main outlines of right and wrong—but only in concrete attainment. The problem was not in knowing the path of virtue but in following it. The task in America was not additions to moral philosophy but an implementation of the most assured certainties of Western moral theory. The need was a society in which men would be both virtuous and happy. Thus, the concern for institutional development, the easy repetition of the conventional doctrines of natural law, and the relative dearth of ethical and esthetic theory.

Yet, whether or not they felt any burden to articulate and rationalize them, the leaders of the American Revolution reflected certain clear preferences. They celebrated a distinctive style of life, and one they assumed to be most conducive to virtue and fulfillment. They best expressed these preferences in the often stilted language of agrarianism, and even occasionally in the more technical jargon of French physiocratic theory. They best demonstrated these preferences by their own careers. Here, in their prevalent conception of the good life, they updated the moral imperatives in Locke's conception of natural property and expressed in a peculiarly secular setting many of the ethical themes of Christianity. Of course, in their idealization of husbandry, in their romantic celebration of life on a farm or in an artisan's shop, they often ignored harsh realities—their own typical involvement in speculative land deals, their zest for unearned increments in a rapidly developing country, their cavalier theft of Indian lands, the embarrassed effort of Southerners to fit Negro slavery into the ideal model, the typical exemption of gentlemen estate owners from the more demanding tasks of the farm, the frequent overlap of agriculture with commercial and financial enterprises, and the common demand, by all groups, for special governmental privileges. The political leaders, almost without exception, were gentlemen farmers, gifted with exceptional abilities, often with inherited wealth or outside sources of income, and more nearly estate managers or businessmen than dirt farmers. They thus idealized what they were not, and cast a romantic glow around what struggling yeomen could never idealize. Even cosmopolitan Franklin, himself a business success in Philadelphia, lauded agriculture, flirted with physiocratic theories, and celebrated the small farmer, even as he engaged in grandiose land speculations in the Ohio valley, undoubtedly hoping to profit from the later hopes and dreams of simple yeomen. Alexander Hamilton, so aware of the promise of finance and manufacturing in assuring national growth and greatness, so willing to see large numbers of people assume a dependent economic role, still paid lip service to the agrarian ideal. He stressed that factory laborers would be seasonal workers or marginal people, such as youth and women, not farm proprietors, and tried to justify manufacturing as a means of strengthening agriculture.

The American celebration of property, in its more ideal expression, was a celebration of independent artistry. On his own farm a man was not dependent on anyone else in the most critical area of economics. He was his own boss and thus, in the rhetoric of natural rights, *free.* He could bring skill, dedication, and hard work to a generally friendly nature, creating not only his subsistence but objects of harmony and beauty. God, said the French physiocrats, alone added His increase to the labor of farmers, making husbandry the only occupation that really added a net increase to the sum of wealth. A farmer was free to fail or to succeed. His tasks had to be largely private. An artist conceives and completes his own tasks in his own private way. If a boss, an intruding community, a government tells him what to do or how to do it he is no longer free but in some sense servile. Free enterprise, and thus free men, preclude any subordinate economic roles. John Adams and James Madison each foresaw a foreboding future for America, for with time extremes of wealth would develop and a growing number of men would be without property, necessarily dependent upon other men for their wages and subsistence. With almost everyone else they deplored such an eventuality, and at times almost despairingly sought ways to postpone it, but still wanted to frame institutions with these dire prospects in mind.

As Jefferson idealized it, independent enterprise on a farm or in a craft served an educational role. It inculcates not only skills but strength of character. With his immense stake in society, with his freedom to defend, the yeoman will be a responsible citizen, immune to popular whims, suspicious of government, jealous of his freedom. If he does not have access to a farm or shop, if he cannot manage the tools of production and reap the rewards of his own labor, he cannot be free. He has to depend on others. Even if he receives good wages he remains servile. After all, a slave may be well fed or indulged with all manner of wonderful consumer goods. Generous treatment may ameliorate his suffering but it cannot justify his slavery. Always there was an easy assumption—economic dependency means some degree of political dependency. Property and political power go together; Adams and Madison were only the most outspoken in emphasizing this commonplace. Jefferson had a twofold fear: of special, monopolistic privilege and of a resulting, nonpropertied laboring class. Both threatened the new republic of virtue, which had to be a republic of independent artisans.

This agrarianism assumes that man finds his highest fulfillment not in consumption, not in charity, not even in delightful social intercourse but in private, creative endeavors. Jefferson even assumed that such fulfillment required the privacy of detached homes. He reacted in horror to the compact, agricultural villages of France. Such living in each others' laps surely reflected some devilish strategy of control by the Catholic church, and in itself helped produce the servile peasants that he observed in so many of the provinces. In America everyone could become an entrepreneur, with esthetic goods fully merged with economic ones. One after the other the heroes of the early republic expressed their yearnings to be back at the plantation. Washington found solace at Mt. Vernon. In his decades of selfless service to his country at home and abroad, John Adams dreamed of his farm at Quincy, and found solace in moments of despair by fantasy calculations of new fields, new orchards, new arrangements of streams and trees. He was the alienated artist, too long removed from his medium. Jefferson, as everyone knows, thirsted for Monticello, and professed his greatest happiness in pursuing his experiments in scientific agriculture or his efforts to beautify his large parklike grounds. Both Madison and Monroe yielded to the lure of land speculation, but they also struggled to build their own Virginia estates.

Even Jefferson, in his concern for privacy and a degree of separation from other people, did not desire isolation and loneliness, and always applauded cooperation and social graces. Individual entrepreneurship, the American norm, meant no escape from communal responsibilities. Just the opposite. It created the calibre of men, the forms of virtue, that made for good citizens and conscientious public service. Such virtue was the ultimate foundation of a liberating social order. Only good men could sustain freedom. Men of sturdy independence, able to perceive the relation of their liberties to that of others, made possible a good republic. Slavery was the greatest threat just here—in the weakening of the character of slave owners. Americans were easily persuaded that the Saxon yeoman of old England had given way to luxury and effeminacy, just as the growing dissipations of the Roman gentry led to the fall of the Roman Republic. It could happen in America. But in 1776 the desired independence from England was not only a justified reaction against tyranny, but a deliberate separation of a still innocent and virtuous America from the developing evils of a stagnant and decaying Europe.

6. *Rights in the American Republic*

I N AMERICA the emphasis upon constitutionalism and the rule
of law has become a cliché. However much the counter-
emphasis upon democracy or upon majority rule, Americans
are at least vaguely aware that the leeway for democratic decision making is strictly circumscribed by constitutional law. So
far the courts have upheld this law and the public has at least
begrudgingly sanctioned it. The concept of natural law—of an
objective moral order, of universal principles of right—was one
of the two main sources of American constitutionalism.

The other source was popular sovereignty. This principle
led to the machinery of popular compacting—to conventions,
ratification procedures, amendment processes. In drafting compacts all the people should participate. The compact itself determines which of the people participate, and to what extent, in the
actual government. In the earliest state governments and in the
federal government established in 1787, the franchised voters
often controlled only one branch of government—the legislature. This limited control quickly changed. States moved to
elected governors and broadened the franchise. At the national
level the party system nullified the intended, nondemocratic
function of both the electoral college and the indirect election of

senators (the Seventeenth Amendment confirmed the change rather than effected it). The "democratization" of American governments disguised the difference beween constitutional process and ordinary legislation. In effect, voters today participate to the same extent in both. Very often they show less interest in and become less involved with constitutional issues, a reverse of the relative importance of the two as dictated by theory. For even now constitutional law has the higher sanction, and both in theory and in legal interpretation controls legislatures. Covenants still outrank statutes.

Written compacts attest to the popular source of governmental authority. If the people are effectively sovereign, they can, in one sense, establish any form of government they wish. They have the physical power to control their own institutions. But do they have the *right* to do as they will? As the preceding chapters show, the answer of Western Christendom was always a resounding "No." If the highest law in a state rested only on the will of the people, albeit expressed in carefully composed and solemn covenants and not in adventitious legislative enactments, then law would still rest on sheer power. Hobbes wins his point, and the state becomes only a positive instrument of the collected will of a people. Those who adhered to natural law sought a higher authority than any people for the most authoritative forms of law. God or nature ordained it. Conventions or congresses may reaffirm it, fit it to particular circumstances, or establish the machinery to enforce it, but they do not create it. In the words of John Adams, magistrates are its ministers, judges its interpreters, and all who want to be free its servants. Laws derive "from the Divinity," and are "silent magistrates, . . . founded on eternal morals, . . . emanations of the Divine Mind." [1]

This celebration of law had two levels of meaning. Adams, like most of his countrymen, knew the importance of clear, written rules in any society. Only in a legal order could one find security. In this sense a rule of law referred, for the most part, to positive law. But in a more lofty sense Adams meant by law those rules that met a moral test, that conformed to right reason and contributed to the proper ends of any society. In this sense, law meant natural law or God's law.

Anyone who would understand politics in eighteenth-century America must have occasional recourse to religious beliefs. Residual forms of Christian theism remained the keystone not only of popular cosmology and ontology (beliefs about the origins of the universe and about the nature of highest reality) but also of the beliefs of the intellectual leaders. It was as difficult to locate an authentic atheist in America as to find anyone who rejected popular sovereignty or natural law. The three all cohere very closely. The confident assurance of an ordered, logical, comprehensible universe rested on the belief in a purposeful creator. Indeed, for many of the celebrated founding fathers, including the three most influential—Adams, Jefferson, and Madison—this theism was in no sense orthodox, and was quite different in some of its implications from that of seventeenth-century Christians. Rational Christians or Deists kept little of Christian belief except the creative principle, a belief in a purposeful universe, an assurance of divine providence or judgment, and usually a hope for personal immortality. In a country already rich with sectarian diversity, few still followed the early Puritans in seeking a body of laws directly out of revealed scripture. God published all the laws necessary for political order in nature, made them available to ordinary human understanding, and placed the needed sanctions in the dire consequences of avoidance or disobedience. The appeal of natural rights was to divine authority, the way God willed all things. But this appeal was not slavish; just the opposite. Almost every influential political theorist from Locke on had assumed divine benevolence or, in Franklin's terms, that God wanted men to be happy and thus gave them the means of happiness. Gone were earlier Calvinist suspicions that, at times, even tyranny represented Godly punishment and that man found redemption only by bending his will to that of God. Thus, the practical appeal of natural rights was to utility, to the realizable benefits of political righteousness, to the greatest good for the greatest number.

In one sense utility was a sufficient vindication of rights.

Surely, if persuaded that one's secure, long-range happiness depended upon the mutual forebearance involved in protected life, liberty, and property, one would give his enthusiastic assent to those principles. But such a vindication seemed terribly vulnerable in the eighteenth century. The expectation of uncoerced rationality was never very high. What eternally is, not men's perilous calculations of self-interest, had to support public order and right.

But, clearly, the appeal to natural rights was not a mere propagandistic strategy. It accurately reflected men's most fervent beliefs even as it served as a rationalization for their political commitments. Of course, in the appeals to nature and God there was, often, an unnoticed bit of condescension toward the common people. In most ways men like Jefferson and Adams were much more pessimistic about mankind than were seventeenth-century Calvinists, who at least balanced concepts of depravity with soaring hopes of redemption. Ordinary people needed a principle of authority to reinforce the dictates of prudence. Thus the paraphrase of Jefferson's much-quoted query: would the people continue to respect the liberties of others if they ceased to believe that these liberties were from God? Not likely. The type of self-discipline and restraint necessary for the rule of law required a belief in firm and effective authority, although a highly abstract authority. This belief moved Jefferson closer to Hobbes than he realized. It also accounted for the general fear of popular atheism. John Adams puzzled over the intellectual dilemmas of theism, read with some appreciation the intellectual arguments of French atheists, but trembled at the prospect of any widespread loss of popular belief in some version of the Christian God. For this belief in a designer and lawmaker almost alone gave to law a status above any mere instrument of human desires.

For a John Adams the very principle of law was rational order. It provided a rule of reason over whim, of truth over fickle opinion, of learned judges over popular assemblies. Allegiance to an objective order of law, anchored in divine will and a support for all hopes for immortality, would check popular passions, restrain the circuslike irresponsibility of elections and factional politics. The idea of a higher law, from this perspective, was mildly elitish. The normal quardians of morality and order, the masters of abstraction, the ministers and professors and lawyers, were its proper interpreters. Established men, those with extensive property and social status, were its prime supporters. But a concept of a higher law had another implication. It not only justified resistance to obvious tyranny, from monarch or mob, but seemed to bestow a special legitimacy to private conscience. Since natural law is a species of moral law, it is the obvious standard of appeal for anyone who feels burdened to challenge the existing order, for pacifists who resist war or abolitionists who try to outlaw slavery. In a stable, consensual social order the principle of law may restrain democratic majorities, provide a refuge for resented minorities, and leaven politics with the wisdom of an intellectual and moral elite. But in a splintered society, with clashing moral opinions, it becomes the principle rationale for disorder and even near anarchy, liberating fanatics more often than it restrains mobs.

As Machiavelli had first suggested, natural rights were not much help in forming new governments. The affirmed ends of life, liberty, and property, at best, indicated a few quite general restrictions on a legitimate government. It could not threaten or take life arbitrarily, with *arbitrary* the critical word awaiting specific content. It could not condone slavery, and had a positive obligation to extend the scope of individual autonomy. It was unclear which specific forms of freedom were necessary to fulfill this commitment. Finally, not only could a government not take one's property without consent, it had a prime obligation to protect private property. But it was less clear what types of property deserved this sacrosanct status, or what form of government would meet the requirement of consent (surely each individual did not have a veto over tax laws). It was difficult to move from natural rights, as a broad ethical mandate, to specific guidelines for a government let alone to a body of concrete laws. Ethical ends too easily lose all their integrity when reduced to maxims of conduct, for the ends have to function in varied situations that cannot be fully anticipated in any detailed formulation of human rights. For this reason the ends have to remain quite general points of reference, vantage points for assessing particular rules in particular contexts. Both in constitutions and in statutes, natural law requires a complex harmonizing of broad ethical commitments, ever changing circumstances, and enforceable rules of law.

Since natural rights are, by definition, unalienable and themselves the reason for having government, they are not properly a product of any covenant or compact. They are the *reason for* covenanting, and properly shape the content of any compact. As natural-rights theorists always emphasized, any irrational attempt to surrender inherent rights, any popular acquiescence in tyranny, even by a solemn compact, was automatically void. Since a people cannot, in a morally valid way, surrender their essential rights to any government, but only the power of enforcing those rights, there is no logical reason for itemizing such reserved rights in a compact of government. In a sense, natural rights are implicitly present in any compact. In fact, there are even dangers in an overly explicit bill of rights. Beyond a general affirmation of life, liberty, and property, any litany of rights has to contain, in effect, only the implicated means for realizing those ends. No list could ever exhaust all the implications or fit the ends in all conceivable situations. At best, such a list instructs those who govern, or remains as a reminder for the people. At worst, a list of rights so legalizes moral principles as to invite casuistic interpretations that violate their very substance.

In a written constitution the only fitting place for an affirmation of natural rights is in the preamble. Here a people can express, in their own special language, the universal ends for which they covenant and the outer limits of governmental power. This location avoids a dilemma. A compact of government reflects not just universal principles but contextual realities. It is what a given people at a given time and place want in the way of government and is amendable at their will. But natural rights are not creatures of compact nor are they subject to any amendment except, possibly, in the language used to express them. If freedom to worship as one chooses is a natural right, then the affirmation of such a right should not be in an amendable article of a constitution, although such a compact might well clarify the ecclesiastical privileges of different religious sects or provide the terms of a religious establishment (assuming that an established church is consistent with freedom of worship, a view that was generally accepted in the eighteenth century).

Most of the original thirteen states did distinguish between a compact and inherent rights. In the two earliest state constitutions, New Hampshire and South Carolina simply delegated specific powers of government and made no mention of reserved rights. With independence, Connecticut legislated a brief resumé of rights as an addition to its retained colonial charter. In enduring precedents, Virginia and Pennsylvania wrote separate declarations of right (Virginia's declaration was a distinct document, approved two days before her compact of government). With only minor changes, Maryland and North Carolina copied the Virginia declaration. Vermont, Massachusetts, and New Hampshire (in her second constitution) all had separate bills of right, with much of the wording borrowed from Virginia and Pennsylvania. The Delaware convention adopted a Declaration of Rights and Fundamental Rules modeled on that of Virginia, and kept it quite distinct from the later plan of government, which also included unamendable procedural rights. New York prefaced her constitution with the Declaration of Independence, thus incorporating Jefferson's brief but classic statement of natural-rights theory. Only Georgia and New Jersey confusingly placed itemized rights in regular, indistinguishable, and apparently amendable articles of their compacts.

The influential Virginia and Pennsylvania declarations were very complex documents. Both began with a ringing affirmation of natural rights, or what amounted to a preamble of ultimate principles. Virginia declared that all men are by nature "equally free and independent," that they have certain inherent rights which, when they enter a state of society, they cannot "by any compact, deprive or divest their posterity, namely the enjoyment of life and liberty, with the means of acquiring and possessing property, and pursuing and obtaining happiness and safety." Pennsylvania abbreviated the phrasing only slightly. It referred to "natural, inherent and unalienable rights," and defined them as "enjoying and defending life and liberty, acquiring, possessing and protecting property, and pursuing and obtaining happiness and safety." Each was clearer and more explicit than Jefferson was in the Declaration. "Equally free and independent" expressed much better the traditional meaning of liberty than "all men are born equal." Virginia was explicit in denying any possible alienation of these rights even by compact. In stressing the means of acquiring and of possessing property, both states gave such a positive meaning to property as to approximate the moral content of Locke's natural property.[2]

Beyond this sweeping statement of principle, all the early declarations included a mixed baggage. Virginia followed the affirmation of natural rights by a strong assertion of popular sovereignty, a defense of the right of revolution, and then by a more general analysis of governmental ends. At places it seemed more of a sermon than a bill of rights. It included homilies on good government, endorsed a separation of governmental functions, suggested a broad franchise (at least as broad as real-property ownership), prescribed free elections, and even advised economy in government finances. Being separate from the constitution, the declaration used the language of obligation, not of mandate. The most detailed sections specified traditional English procedural safeguards: arrest only for cause, a speedy trial, confrontation by accusers, an impartial jury in all cases, unanimous conviction, no self-incrimination, no excessive bails or punishments, and no search without cause and warrant. A final section affirmed freedom of conscience in religion. It did not, in itself, dissolve the existing establishment, provide equality for all sects, or remove existing disabilities in office holding based on religion or the lack of it. Only in 1786 did Jefferson's famous Bill of Religious Freedom finally abolish most forms of religious preference in Virginia.

The Pennsylvania Declaration and Plan of Government, jointly, made up the state constitution. As a preface to the constitution, the declaration mandated rights and, presumably, had a more binding legal status than the one in Virginia. Its second section declared it a "natural and unalienable right" to be able to worship Almighty God according to the dictates of conscience, and specifically excluded any established church, although it backhandedly endorsed a form of theism. It emphasized popular sovereignty and the right of revolution, specifically required consent in the taking of property, and gave special protection to pacifists and those who would take no oaths. It contained almost the same language as that of Virginia in its reiteration of common-law procedural protections.

In most respects the New England bills of right varied only in minor details. John Adams was able to expand the length in Massachusetts by adding a great deal more legal jargon. Reflecting its prerevolutionary controversies, Massachusetts specified rights of assembly as well as press, urged life-tenured judges, stressed the citizen's right to bear arms, and recommended regular elections. The one basic difference in New England was religious. Each of the three states which wrote constitutions in the revolutionary period (New Hampshire, Vermont, and Massachusetts) affirmed freedom of conscience. But each also provided for the public support of religious worship. Massachusetts, in language weighted with the past, made it the duty as well as the right of each man, publicly and at stated seasons, to worship the Supreme Being according to the dictates of his own conscience. But the happiness of the people and the good order of civil government depended on piety, religion, and morality, and those in turn depended on public worship. Thus, the declaration of rights gave the legislature the authority to require towns to use public taxes to pay ministers and support public worship services, and even to pass laws enjoining attendance at such services, provided only that each person could, if he had his own church separate from the one of the parish, designate his taxes for its support. Baptists in particular fought in vain against this mild establishment, the most controverted section in the declaration. This provision, in milder form, even survived the constitutional revision of 1820. The legal establishment ended only in 1833. New Hampshire and Vermont both copied the Massachusetts provision, but their legislatures never implemented such a full establishment. Neither did Connecticut after adopting her first constitution in 1818, although it contained much of the language in the Massachusetts constitution.[3]

In all the early bills of right the preeminent concern seemed to be procedural safeguards and not vast new horizons of private expression. Most of the early declarations specified freedom of the press, meaning at a minimum a prohibition against prior restraint or official censorship. Such affirmations in themselves did not preclude a wide array of common-law penalties for malicious or irresponsible publications, since the states continued the common law and its severe penalties for criminal or seditious libel. Even such later symbols of free expression as Jefferson and Madison desired some test of responsibility, and supported common-law prosecutions at the state level. The crusade against prior restraint went back to Milton and Locke, although both accepted severe legal penalties for scandalous libels or seditious attacks against duly constituted political authorities. The practical issue in eighteenth-century America was not licensing and prior censorship but a continued controversy over prosecutions after the effect, a controversy which dated from the unsuccessful prosecution of John Peter Zenger in 1733.

The Zenger case and widely publicized arguments in his defense made freedom of the press an issue of popular concern. In effect, a local jury refused to convict Zenger on the legally unprecedented grounds that he told the truth about an unjust colonial government. In English law truth had never vindicated malicious attacks and in some cases only worsened the crime. Benjamin Franklin and other publishers jumped to the defense of this expanded conception of freedom. They republished or plagiarized an influential English defense of an expanded meaning of freedom in *Cato's Letters*, a series of essays written after 1720 by John Trenchard and Thomas Gordon, and possibly the single most important vehicle for carrying British libertarian ideas to America. The effect of this public airing of the issue was at least some degree of confusion over what both freedom of the press and of speech really meant. But, legally, the states could only incorporate an expanded meaning by specific language in their constitutions and, notably, none did so before 1790.

Whatever the meaning, freedom of speech and press had a strong emotional appeal by 1776, insuring appropriate clauses in the state constitutions. The absence of any protection for a free press was one of the most frequent objections to the federal Constitution of 1787 and helped assure its prominent place in the First Amendment. The first constitutional break came in Pennsylvania's new constitution of 1790, and was quickly imitated in Delaware and Kentucky. Pennsylvania, in effect, affirmed the Zenger precedent. It opened the way for "responsible" criticism by the press of official conduct. It provided that anyone prosecuted for such criticism could plead truth as evidence, and that in libel trials the jury could determine both the law and the fact of the case.[4]

It was quite appropriate that Pennsylvania took the lead in this area. At the time of the Revolution the thirteen states varied in their degree of cultural and religious homogeneity. The New England states, Rhode Island excepted, still vainly pursued the Puritan dream of cohesive, unified, harmonious, ordered, and exclusive communities. The continued church establishment testified to this dream. These states carefully continued, in their new charters, the cultural heritage of the old. They wanted a state government closely tied to the provincial towns, and emphasized a broad franchise and frequent elections. They feared what they had suffered aplenty—religious and political factionalism and the excesses of democracy. When John Adams drafted the Massachusetts constitution, he did not want any license for irresponsible behavior, any charter for political parties, any undiscriminating tolerance for all forms of error and foolishness, any encouragement of popular demagogues. He wanted no expanded conception of free speech or free press. But states such as Pennsylvania inherited a more pluralistic society, and reflected the necessities of the situation in granting religious equality to all sects and in special provisions for conscientious objectors. Pennsylvania was already a state made up of diverse creeds and life styles, ranging from the Quakers of Philadelphia and the Amish and Mennonites of the Susquehanna valley to the raucous Scotch-Irish of the frontier. The state government had to accept added restraints on its power to enforce uniformity or to create a homogeneous whole, but it did not assume any positive power to intervene in local, exclusive communities to protect minority rights. The expanded range of freedom entailed no celebration of pluralism but a necessary adjustment to a growing diversity in America and the need to accommodate this diversity through added restraints and a broader range of accepted options at each ascending level of political organization. This accommodation of diversity culminated, both logically and in fact, in the Bill of Rights added to the federal Constitution.

The delegates at Philadelphia in 1787 did not add their generalities to the litany of natural rights or embellish their plan of government with a separate bill of rights. That did not mean that the delegates opposed traditional natural rights or expected the new federal government to usurp them. The strong support for a new federal government derived, in large part, from a fear for liberty in America and particularly from fears of the corrosive dangers to property posed by popular majorities. The delegates favored liberty and the secure order necessary for its preservation, and feared the excesses of democracy which always threaten freedom. Except for compromises on slavery, the convention was prolibertarian, again with property perceived as the most fundamental of all rights. The need was for a federal government powerful enough to protect liberty from enemies at home and abroad.

There was no fight over grand principles of government. The delegates easily assumed those and quickly bogged down on the main agenda—a new frame of government. The hazards here were immense, and when the delegates finally weathered all the divisive controversies and completed a halfway acceptable document they could only marvel at their own handiwork. At the very end of this ordeal, for such it was, George Mason urged the addition of a bill of rights to the preamble. The delegates apparently recognized that as a can of worms; the ensuing efforts at wording might have wrecked the whole enterprise. John Sherman pointed out that the new federal Constitution in no way repealed state declarations of rights, and clearly wanted to drop the issue. Without a dissenting vote, and only one abstention, the convention voted against adding a bill of rights. A related motion to add a provision on the freedom of the press also lost in confrontation with the simple argument that the power of the new government did not extend that far.[5]

Despite the absence of a separate bill of rights the new constitution incorporated a few of the procedural safeguards of common law. In establishing the legislative powers of the new Congress, the convention occasionally turned from positive delegation to negative limits: *habeas corpus* "shall not be suspended"; "No bill of attainder or *ex post facto* laws shall be passed." In the section creating the federal judiciary it also stipulated jury trial. These provisions were alone reiminiscent of the state declarations.

In the *Federalist Papers* Alexander Hamilton accepted the difficult task of defending the original draft against what had become the most telling criticism—the lack of a bill of rights. By this time it was almost certain that ratification would lead to a bill of rights in the form of amendments, as leading proponents of the Constitution, including Madison, had promised, and at least three states ratified with that as an understood condition. Still, Hamilton conceded nothing. He insisted that the most important rights were already in the document. In an opposite tack, he correctly argued that the British heritage of written guarantees—in Magna Charta, the Petition of Right, and the Bill of Rights—involved covenants wrung from ruling princes and had no relationship to constitutions established by a sovereign people who specifically delegated certain powers. In fact, the whole Constitution, if ratified by the people, would be as much a bill of rights as the British examples. Hamilton even argued, as did other "Federalists," that a list of reserved rights could be dangerous to liberty, for such a negative denial of power might somehow suggest a prior grant and thus reduce individual rights by opening the whole issue to legal subtleties. Finally, even the state declarations of such rights as freedom of the press were almost meaningless in themselves. What is the liberty of the press and who defines it? Ultimately, said Hamilton, respect for such freedoms rests not on verbal declarations but on public opinion and the respect of a people for the rights of others.[6]

Inundated with amendment proposals from most of the states, the new federal Congress compressed them into twelve and submitted them to the states, which ratified the ten now known as the Bill of Rights. The amendments served two related but often divergent purposes: to limit federal power in relation to the states and to protect individual rights against usurpation by the new federal government. The Tenth Amendment, and for the most part the celebrated First, limited federal prerogatives as against the states. The Ninth reserved all unspecified rights to the people, an almost meaningless testimony to the inability of any list to comprehend all the moral ends of government. The concluding section of the Fifth Amendment clearly affirmed the doctrine of natural rights. It prevented the federal government from depriving any person "of life, liberty, or property, without due process of law," and the taking of private property for public uses without just compensation. This section, in effect, incorporated the moral tenor of the Declaration of Independence and by logic should have been a part of the preamble.

Several articles or parts of them guaranteed the procedural protection itemized in most state declarations. They extended jury provisions; prohibited double jeopardy, self-incrimination, and excessive or cruel punishments; required confrontation by accusers; and gave defendants the right to compel witnesses. Articles II and III protected the citizen's right to bear arms and prohibited quartering except in time of war. Article IV forbade illegal searches and seizures and set strict rules for warrants. These English procedures applied only to federal courts, and in effect brought these courts into conformity with most state courts. Since the listed rights denied powers not granted in the original Constitution, it is difficult to assess their early importance in our system. Perhaps they mainly appeased public apprehensions. But the Bill of Rights had a large future. The Fourteenth Amendment transformed its provisions into guarantees and pushed them into the forefront of constitutional litigation in the twentieth century.

The First Amendment, which later came to symbolize individual rights, figured in the first major controversy involving constitutional rights. It denied any power to the federal Congress to make laws respecting an establishment of, or preventing the free exercise of, religion, or any laws abridging the freedom of speech, press, petition, or peaceful assembly. This wording, despite the probable intent of Congress in drafting it, did not clearly prevent Congress from passing any laws relating to religion, and surely did not contain the later idea of complete separation. It did express a form of federal neutrality. The states might have established churches (as in New England), and of different varieties, but all would be equal at the federal level. At the time most states had some legal preference for Christians, Protestants, theists, or even trinitarians. The federal convention had scrupulously avoided this issue in its oath for the president and in its explicit repudiation of religious oaths for federal officials.

More crucial at the time, the amendment only said that Congress could not pass laws *abridging* freedom of the press, speech, petition, and assembly. It left open the unintended possibility of laws that regulated or expanded these freedoms. The rather obvious congressional intent had been to reserve laws touching these issues to the states, and to exclude the federal government completely, since the original Constitution granted no powers at all over the press. Hamilton proved prophetic. By their effort to restrict the federal government from entering a field where it had no delegated powers, the amending states in fact opened up such new possibilities of federal action as the Sedition Act of 1798. Also, by its language, the amendment restricted Congress, not the president or the federal courts. Even before the Sedition Act, the executive branch secured two indictments for seditious libel in federal courts, acting under assumed common-law authority. Admittedly, this action in no way rested on interpretations of the First Amendment, but one possible justification of it was the fact that it was quite consistent with the First Amendment, since it involved no congressional action and no federal law.

The Sedition Act seemed, to Jeffersonian Republicans, a clear violation of the First Amendment. It was clearly a federal law affecting speech and press, and its acknowledged purpose was to silence criticism of the Adams administration and the federal government. But Federalists emphasized that it expanded the range of meaning in freedom of speech and press rather than *abridged* it. Unlike common-law definitions still in use at the state level and even in federal courts, it followed Pennsylvania in demanding libelous intent and in making truth an allowable defense. In actual operation, and before largely Federalist judges, this protection proved empty, for in the inflamed context of partisan political speeches and editorials truth was hard to identify, and prosecutors in effect forced defendants to "prove" truthfulness, reversing the normal obligation of proof. But the Federalist argument still stood—the act in no clear way abridged freedom as heretofore defined. The strongest legal claim for Republicans was that English common law did not apply at the federal level, an argument extensively developed by Madison in his defense of the Virginia Resolutions. If it did not apply, then any federal law in any way restricting freedom of press or speech would be automatically unconstitutional because there would be no prior standard for comparison. Eventually, in a libel action brought against opponents of Jefferson under common-law jurisdiction, the Supreme Court ruled that there was no common law of crimes at the federal level, but that was not until 1812. Had the Sedition Act come before the Supreme Court during its brief career (it expired in 1801 and President Jefferson suspended all pending prosecutions), there seems little likelihood that the Federalist judges would have declared it unconstitutional. [7]

The Alien and Sedition Acts led to an impassioned war of words reminiscent of the earlier struggle with Britain. Three issues intertwined—the place of parties or factions in the new republic, the boundaries between federal and state jurisdiction, and the rightful scope of expressive freedoms in a society. The Federalist defenders of the Sedition Act were often egotistic and overly sensitive political partisans, but they were not enemies of popular sovereignty and natural rights. Some of them, including President Adams, had been and remained eloquent advocates of both. They simply decried what they conceived as irresponsible and demagogic license, a license that placed all government, all order, and all protected freedoms in jeopardy. Adams still reflected the Calvinist idealization of magistrates and the Puritan concern for social solidarity. He wanted the proper respect for a duly constituted government and the proper veneration for honest and honorable public servants, of which he was one. Without this respect and deference, he feared, popular government, based on consent and instructed by frequent elections, would degenerate into factionalism and anarchy. Genteel criticism and political debate were desirable, but the corrosive vilification of his administration and of him personally threatened to throw the new, vulnerable national government into contempt at home and weaken it in critical negotiations abroad. He spoke in an atmosphere of near war. The Republicans, the party in opposition, faced with a legal harassment that won them votes but inflicted a cruel punishment on editors and a few politicians, appealed to the rights of speech and press, and by their very circumstances had to embrace the more extreme libertarian definition of these rights. They also turned Federalist prosecutions under the act into evidence of the truth of their most extreme political attacks. Obviously, in this context, much of their emphasis upon principle reflected little more than partisan strategy. Once in power the Republicans rarely hesitated to indict for libel under the common law. But mixed with self-interest were some new and probing analyses of the place of expressive freedoms in a republican society.

The Republicans had one unifying position—that the Sedition Act violated the First Amendment by illegally expanding the area of federal jurisdiction. They emphasized the "no law" part of the amendment, not the qualification of "abridgement." Jefferson and Madison, in the Kentucky and Virginia Resolutions, exploited this state-rights theme and claimed for the states the right to determine the constitutionality of federal acts. The complicity of federal judges in the enforcement of the act also helped strengthen Jefferson's suspicions of the courts and led to a later vendetta against one justice, Samuel Chase.

Finally, the controversy over seditious libel began a gradual expansion of permissible criticism of government. The usual arguments in behalf of expanded freedom were practical, at the level of public policy but not at the level of natural law. In America an informed electorate became a vital necessity in good government. In the political arena a bit of give and take was necessary for this education to take place. Here, as Madison conceded, even the test of truth was meaningless, impossible to determine or prove. Besides, a popular government, resting on the sovereignty of the people, was a servant and not a master. Seditious libel was impossible in this circumstance, for the citizens were not subjects and no government official was superior to citizens. Such an extreme view of freedom did not win immediate acceptance in law, but in the new century both state and federal governments, by constitutional changes or judicial decision, slowly assimilated and generously applied the idea of truth and good intent as the sole requirements in criticism of public officials. In the twentieth century the courts finally dropped most of these requirements.[8]

The controversy over the Alien and Sedition Acts revealed some of the open-endedness of natural-right theories. As Vattel recognized, the specific demands of life, liberty, and property vary immensely according to social context. What one man may perceive as slavery in one society will appear normal if not liberating in another. The diversity of America, the vast geographical differences, the divergence of state experiences and traditions, required large areas of protected private expression at the federal level. In 1800, despite Jefferson's fears, the federal government was not the source of most threats to individual expression in worship, in the management of property, and in speech and press. At the national level, as Madison suggested in another context, that very diversity precluded dominance by any one sect. No narrow ideology could gain and hold the power of a national majority. But majorities did dominate local affairs. Here was where natural-right theories or constitutional guarantees often meant almost nothing, at least not until local minorities gained some visibility, some leverage in state or national affairs. Even many of the vaunted supports of liberty, such as jury trial, armed rather than restrained local majorities, although they did protect such majorities from the power of governments. The trouble was, often, that the distant federal government, reflecting a broad moral consensus, upheld accepted principles of justice much more often than did local majorities. A coercive democracy, not a profound respect for individual autonomy, usually prevailed in the provinces.

But to describe is not to judge. Here competing values lead men to different estimates. Maybe a form of local totalitarianism is not an unmitigated evil. Maybe it is not only inevitable but desirable. Perhaps the most meaningful freedom in nineteenth-century America was just the freedom, in the large diversity and with the great openings to the west, to find one's own intolerant community and to adhere to it without external supervision and there to develop a secure sense of identity within its restrictive beliefs and mores. Maybe the idea of freedom, almost unnoticed, can become an excuse for blanket toleration, for an acceptance of any and all differences, and not a discerning respect for the minimal conditions of human fulfillment. It is easy on natural-rights grounds to condemn all forms of exclusion from nature, all efforts to deprive men of the fruit of their labor, all forms of slavery, but exceedingly difficult to deduce any single standard for expressive freedoms. In some contexts, unlimited freedom of self-expression might threaten not only order but also any secure sense of identity, any way of discriminating among competing beliefs, any moral discrimination or sensitivity at all, any possibility of a fulfilling community. The difficult issue may well be determining the right context for exclusivity and intolerance, not the problem of eliminating these "evils." Thus, even for some individuals, the most valued freedom of all may be the freedom to become part of a secure and very sectarian community, safe from external controls over the internal regimen and free to expel all subversive elements within. In practical terms, this freedom includes the right of Amish parents not to send their children to public schools, of bishops to censor church publications, of youthful communes to expel ideological revisionists, of purely private clubs to use any arbitrary criterion they wish to limit membership.

In this perspective, Americans did well in 1791 to try in every possible way to restrain the large centers of power in behalf of local versions of righteousness or privilege, rather than creating a centralized leviathan with the power to enforce upon regions and localities some cosmopolitan standard of right or some national forms of privilege. This strategy precluded any vast, continental tyranny (or any national reign of "justice"). It left dissenting minorities, such as the angry Baptists of Massachusetts, chafing under what they perceived as a very unfair and discriminatory church establishment. But in an empire of liberty, in a federation of quite diverse communities, the saving grace was the right to move on. The Baptists could move to Pennsylvania, admittedly not without great personal sacrifice, but move they could, and with full federal protection for their right to enter another state without fee and for their right to move their property without special assessments. Somewhere, in the states and territories, almost any group could find an isolated haven even for the most daring social experiments, always with the consoling assurance that, at the least, no threats to their local autonomy originated at the imperial center.

Negroes made up the one glaring exception. Here the federal government was a party to a local violation of an obvious natural right, and not only complicitous in the usual and inescapable sense of nonintervention in local affairs, but also in the unique, positive sense of incorporating slavery into the federal Constitution and providing several forms of federal protection for this form of local "property." Negro slaves, unlike other minorities, were not citizens and could not move on. The federal government did not even have unambiguous constitutional authority to prevent slavery in its own territories, and in several cases (such as fugitive slave laws) intruded itself into free states and local jurisdictions to maintain the institution.

It is hard to grasp how radically the context of rights in America has changed since 1790. The purpose of the original Bill of Rights was to help restrict federal power to problems of national concern and to exclude it almost completely from purely local issues. Thus, the federal government could not establish a church; the states could. It could not restrict freedom of the press; the states could. But in time the unique plight of Negro slaves and the unique federal complicity in slavery gained national attention and concern, even as more and more people thought of the United States as one large community, one indivisible national entity. In the wake of a civil war that, in the perspective of the North, maintained the nation, the federal government took on a new responsibility—guaranteeing the rights of blacks at the state level. It could do so only by usurpation or by a new grant of constitutional power, which it attained by the Fourteenth Amendment. This constitutional revolution, as fundamental as the ratification of the federal Constitution of 1787, made life, liberty, and property a federal promise and not merely a restriction on federal power. The federal government, in behalf of individuals, could now intrude directly into the states or, more accurate at this point, into the major administrative subdivisions of one unified sovereign nation. Only slowly did Congress and the federal courts implement this constitutional revolution, thus muting its popular impact. After the rapid waning of enthusiasm for Negro rights, the federal courts first used the protection clause of the Fourteenth Amendment to secure the "property" rights (clearly not a form of natural property) of corporate persons, and only after 1920 did it consistently use it to incorporate practically the whole Bill of Rights under the blanket of federal power. This incorporation, in turn, gave constitutional leeway for a wide range of libertarian legislation in behalf of Negroes and women.

For most of our national history the federal government has not been the principal enemy of individual or minority-group rights. The Alien and Sedition Acts did not establish an enduring precedent. Of course, in one sense, the federal government by its inaction was often complicitous in local forms of repression, but its inaction until after 1868 was consistent with its constitutional mandate. By the twentieth century the federal government became, in fact, the most secure guardian of those rights that seemed most important to men of power and moral influence, and which seemed most endangered, and which were most often the source of litigation. Notably, areas such as criminal procedures, equal treatment, and the expressive freedoms (religion, press, speech, assembly) received the most attention. Other traditional rights, including the broadest and most vital of all, such as the natural right of property (meaning the right to own, manage, and receive the full returns from the means of production, and emphatically not such personal or corporate privileges as possessing and trading in money, consumer goods, or capital investments), not only failed to receive legal recognition but practically dropped from public awareness or concern.

In the twentieth century, the federal government, in response to appeals for relief from aggrieved citizens, has often forced reluctant local majorities to honor constitutional rights and to live up to all the procedural demands of due process. The federal courts have used the rule of law, and presumptively of "right," as a direct challenge to the expressed will of the people in varied political units. This role is in every sense undemocratic, for it restricts local majorities and, at times, clearly challenges or moves ahead of majority opinion in the nation as a whole, thus eliciting the same opposition from the president or Congress as from local governments. These conflicts are all understandable, for at least in most parochial contexts the democratic will, for better or worse, is narrow, exclusive, and very intolerant, even though by some standard of evaluation also "true" and "right." Judges obviously vindicate their libertarian decisions by appeal not to their superior wisdom but to the Fourteenth Amendment and to the original Bill of Rights. The courts have to apply the Constitution and thus implement the mature, long-term commitments of the people. These commitments are just what the people, in particular concrete situations and in local contexts or in the stress and strain of the moment, often forget or repudiate. But, in another sense, the judges cannot avoid exemplifying an inherent aspect of the whole natural-law tradition, or of any attempt to maintain an allegedly moral check upon either governmental power or upon informal modes of social control. Someone has to decipher the will of God, read correctly the structure of nature, decipher fairly the minimal and universal conditions of human happiness, or, more pertinent today, read correctly the enduring, consensual will of the people. And in fact and by necessity a special class of men always do most of this interpreting, whether it be flaming prophets, scholarly priests, learned lawyers, or honored judges.

Ironically, the tremendous expansion of federal power in all areas, including the expanded role in protecting individual rights, has finally transformed the often fantastic eighteenth-century fears of a federal leviathan into prophetic admonitions. Battled and bloodied into submission to, if not acceptance of, minimal national standards, the local political bastions of suppression will probably never regain their former, *de facto* sovereignty. The environment challenges them much more than the courts. In the great boiling mix of American society, consensual communities are losing their geographic definition. But the need they serve remains. Thus they have become affinity groups in a spatially pluralistic society. These groups may, with justice, demand more autonomy, more decentralized roles, and thus more internal power to enforce their own standards (however arbitrary and even cruel they seem to outsiders) upon their members. There may be, in other words, a strong reaction to national uniformity and homogeneity, but it will probably not take the form of enduring local, politically secure, geographical enclaves, but will assume a more sectarian aspect and will mean a growing distrust of government at all levels.

With federal power dominant, with the vast federal government responsive to so many powerful constituencies, including embittered minorities with virtually unlimited demands, the federal government is now the most likely source of major abuses of power, of unintentional or deliberate efforts to coerce and control citizens, to reduce their sphere of private choice. More perplexing, it may often threaten individual freedom in the very pursuit of justice, destroy liberty in the very effort to diminish intolerance. In any case, such a center of power, with all its newly won ability to protect and even guarantee liberty, at least as the custodians of power define it, has finally enough power to destroy liberty, at least as suffering misfits may define it. In this perspective, our founding fathers were wise in trying to restrain positive government by traditional moral guidelines, and possibly wiser than we think in their emphasis upon restraint than upon centralized guarantees.

PART THREE

BALANCED SEPARATION

The Form of Government

᠃᠃᠃᠃᠃᠃᠃᠃᠃᠃᠃᠃᠃᠃᠃᠃᠃᠃᠃᠃᠃᠃᠃᠃᠃᠃᠃

7. *Mixture & Separation*

The Complex Legacy

As JOHN ADAMS ONCE NOTED, newly independent Americans were not adept in the science of government. They were better moral philosophers. They almost unanimously concurred in the general principle that a government gained all its authority from the people, and quickly implemented this principle in unprecedented techniques of drafting, ratifying, and amending constitutions. They easily agreed on life, liberty, and property as the moral ends of any just government, and translated this agreement into lofty preambles or detailed declarations of right. Issues of ultimate authority and purpose, by their very generality, by their abstract simplicity, by their firm roots in Western Christianity, allowed at least a verbal harmony, however many troublesome conflicts still hid behind ambiguities of language.

None of this abstract clarity guided the architects of early American governments. It could not. Given a constancy of ends and a diversity of contexts, a good government had to vary from place to place and from one people to another. Even such a formalist as John Adams conceded this element of relativity. To protect liberty a government had to possess enough power and efficiency to maintain order but not enough power to threaten individual freedom. Any particular government had to exist somewhere between the poles of anarchy and despotism, and the exact position on a broad continuum depended, in large part, on highly variable circumstances. In the context of the American Revolution the earliest concern was more effective restraints on government. By the federal convention of 1787 this consideration was at least in part balanced by a growing concern for effective government and fears of popular anarchy or majoritarian tyranny. But even then the problem of restraint and limits seemed most important.

The colonial experience in government was by far the most important determinant of new forms after independence. The earliest conventions continued more colonial institutions than they usually recognized, and even where they tried to make corrective changes they soon found that they had fallen into new difficulties. Almost as influential were American perceptions of the British form of government, at least in an earlier purity. It was the best historical example of a government resting upon popular consent and designed to safeguard freedom. Beyond these dear lessons of experience and example, most articulate students of government professed at least a general belief in certain necessary attributes of any limited government. The key words were balance and separation, but these words had a wide range of meaning. To search out those meanings is to pursue concepts much more elusive than popular sovereignty or natural rights.

The veneration of some form of governmental balance or equilibrium as a protection against tyranny was a very ancient doctrine. Hinted at by Plato, rather clearly recommended by Aristotle, almost deified by Polybius, the classic idea of balance involved not the functions of government, but the proper mix of classes or estates and of their appropriate governmental expression—monarchy, aristocracy, and democracy. A much more modern tool of limited government—the separation of powers or of such governmental functions as legislation, execution, and adjudication—did not mature until the eighteenth century. Although often celebrated in America, complete separation was almost impossible in practice. In its place, Americans borrowed ideas of checks and balances from a still ascendant idea of a mixed government, which lost much of its logic in America, and used them to modify and transform the principle of separation.

Aristotle permanently shaped political nomenclature by his analytical distinctions. He classified three simple types of constitution in their optimum form—monarchy, aristocracy, and constitutional or popular government—and also in their degenerate and self-serving forms—tyranny, oligarchy, and democracy. Aristotle admitted the appeal of a supremely virtuous monarch or of an aristocracy of true philosopher kings, but doubted the availability of such paragons. In their place he sought means of reconciling all three simple forms of government, and of harmonizing wealth and poverty, civic virtue and selfishness, oligarchy and democracy. In a balanced government of law he placed particular reliance on the middle classes, but never tried to prescribe one best form of government for all types of communities. Each form fits particular circumstances.

The Greek historian and philosopher Polybius turned the idea of mixed government into a compelling doctrine. He did it in defense of the Roman republic, and as a result joined Cicero as the most prominent classical voice in revolutionary America. As Polybius defined it, and as most later writers understood it, a mixed government includes all three simple forms and harmonizes the otherwise divergent interests of the few (aristocracy) and the many (democracy). The principle of unity (monarchy) helps maintain the balance and provides the efficiency and force needed at the head of a government. The three branches in no

sense reflect distinct governmental roles, although the monarchical element will normally carry out what we today call the executive function.[1]

In the high middle ages, Thomas Aquinas revived the idea of
mixed government and used it as a minor chord in his challenge
to absolutism. He set an enduring precedent. Calvin expressed
the same preference, as did most of his followers. In fact, almost
every libertarian spokesman from the Reformation on saw a
mixed government as a valuable safeguard against tyranny. The
details varied, but they usually sought both popular and aristocratic checks on monarchical power, or a balancing of the estates
of the realm. The evolving British government seemed the best
example of mixture, with legislative power shared by a limited
monarch, the hereditary lords, and an elected commons. Practically, the most obvious implication of a mixed government was
a complex legislature, usually a class-based, bicameral assembly
and veto rights for the chief magistrate. Such a mix, alone,
could reflect the common interest of a community and frustrate
laws that catered to distinct elements or classes. The very synonym of tyranny was an imbalance in the state, an ascendancy
of one element over another, such as the poor robbing from the
nobility or the nobility exploiting the peasants. The idea of balance and concurrence did not mean any severe limitations upon
effective and extensive governmental action, but only insured
that the laws enforced by the magistrates did reflect the broadest
possible consensus.

The two revolutions in seventeenth-century England, with
the resulting explosion of political theory, stimulated new appeals to mixed government from all sides. At first the problem
seemed an overly arbitrary government under James I and the
suppression of the normal balance provided by the two houses
of Parliament. But Charles I used the same principle to protest
the pretentions of the Long Parliament, insisting quite correctly
that the idea of balance required monarchical concurrence in all
legislation. In the wake of the Restoration and new threats of
monarchical dominance, Algernon Sidney appealed to the idea

of a proper mix, and grandiloquently asserted that "there never was a good government in the world, that did not consist of the three simple species of monarchy, aristocracy, and democracy . . . ," for only in such a mixed government could all groups participate according to their quality and merit.[2]

Of all the English celebrants of mixed government, James Harrington was the most influential in America. He elaborately developed the idea in his intriguing mixture of utopian dreaming and hardheaded political analysis, *Oceana*. This imaginary commonwealth was particularly appealing to Americans, for it was a nation of farmers and agrarian to its core. More than any of his predecessors, Harrington equated property with power. In such an agricultural state land was virtually the sole source of power. Harrington believed that all countries have a natural aristocracy—men of superior talent, greater ambition or craftiness, or compelling charisma. Implicit in *Oceana*, and quite explicit in John Adams, its leading American admirer, was the one inevitable result of such inequalities of talent. In a free society, and particularly in one that protects private property, advantage will usually win out. A free society assures peaks of achievement and large accumulations of wealth, which lead to large concentrations of political power. It is in this sense that a libertarian social order, in direct contrast to an equalitarian one, not only does not eliminate all forms of nobility but continuously replenishes a class of able and powerful men. Since America decisively rejected all forms of nobility based on birth and title, Adams saw very clearly that American aristocracy would depend primarily upon property. Some men would become wealthy even as others sunk into deeper poverty. Harrington, still captive to the artificial class divisions of England, all too easily described a bipolar division of property between a gentry with large estates and simple yeomen with small farms. Even John Adams fell into this disjunctive pattern, and seemed to ignore the American reality—a continuum of estates from small to very large.

To prevent forms of servility and slavery for a propertyless class of men, Harrington tried to assure a universal, but ob-

viously not an equal, distribution of land, and devised elaborate
agrarian laws to this end (laws requiring equal descent and limiting the size of estates). For the same purpose, he tried to insure
equal power in Oceana for the two main interest groups, the
large- and small-property owners. Guided by their leader and
eventual king, the people of Oceana established a complicated,
mixed constitution, with a deliberative senate of noblemen, who
proposed all new laws, and a huge assembly of complexly
elected delegates from the simple people. They did not debate
but heard speeches by the senators and voted upon all the laws
the senate proposed. The executive head of the state provided a
balancing center of power. Harrington expected this system,
which protected all interests, to eventuate in good laws, which
in turn make good men. He had no confidence in any form of
paternalism, in any king or aristocracy that, without the balancing effect of countervailing power, would ever consistently serve
the national interest against its own private interests. The gentry
may have an excess of talent, of learning, even of wisdom, but
they never have an excess of virtue. All men have passions as
well as powers of reason. Without institutional checks and balances one can never rely on the ascendancy of reason. Because
of their very abilities, the nobles are particularly dangerous. For
this reason, a carefully devised and mixed government is all-important in shaping human behavior. It alone can channel men's
egotistic energies into the paths of virtue and public good. Any
unmixed constitution, any simple form of government, is an invitation to tyranny.[3]

Harrington anticipated many of the challenges and dilemmas
of small agricultural republics in America. He foresaw countries
divided not between the propertied and the unpropertied but
between the divergent interests of large property holders and
small ones. The dilemma of freedom, and particularly the freedom to accumulate large estates, is the early likelihood of monopoly, and foreclosed access rights for increasing numbers of
individuals. The crucial task is to sustain open opportunities and
yet allow effort and ability to flower in superior achievement.

But how restrain the able and rich? The answer, to Harrington, was clearly not just a broad franchise but rather an effective, realized equality of power for the yeomen. Unless checked, the rich and able will not only influence voting but will also dominate popular assemblies. Not only does their wealth give them power, but the very abilities that led to the wealth will also increase their influence over other men. Without the institutional trick, without mechanisms of equilibrium, the rich will quickly monopolize property and power and in effect enslave the majority, who, without property, are neither free nor happy. Forms of simple democracy always prepare the way for such slavery. Or, an equally gloomy alternative, the exploited poor will finally, out of desperation, use their one remaining asset—numbers and sheer physical strength—to overturn the rich, not only appropriating their wealth but extinguishing most of the talent and wisdom possessed by the society.

Harrington sensed that the problem, a most difficult one, was somehow to keep the power of the rich few equal to that of the collection of small entrepreneurs. Thus, he had two strategies—agrarian laws and mixed government—in order to maintain an equality between property and power. What Americans rarely imitated was his economic weapon. Jefferson not only gloried in the repeal of entail and primogeniture, but in Virginia advocated restraints on large estates and recommended homesteads for all families. Few heeded his advice. The vast frontier provided a lame excuse for unlimited accumulation. Later, education, votes for all, and reasonably good chances for employment and consumptive delights became a substitute for the early American commitment to universal entrepreneurial opportunities.

In many ways a mixed constitution reflected European and not American realities. Despite a rather clear distinction between gentlemen and simple men, and widespread popular deference to wealth, family status, and leadership abilities, colonial America never possessed a titled nobility and never had sharp and fast lines between social classes. It reflected a continuum of classes and wealth. There seemed little likelihood that men of wealth and influence would ever accept any isolation in some American version of the House of Lords. Besides, even in Britain, the Lords ill reflected the actual distribution of wealth and power, and ambitious lords certainly did not restrict their political efforts to that one chamber. Whatever the abstract merits of mixed government, it rarely matched the complex array of interests in any modern state. The most realistic effort to implement it in America ignored the bipolar class division; in Massachusetts and other states a few large property owners proposed two legislative assemblies, one apportioned and elected on the basis of sheer numbers, the other on the basis of property. But this plan would never have isolated wealth in one equal chamber, and in all likelihood would have abetted the efforts of the rich to secure predominant power in the state.

Despite its abstract and formalistic qualities, and despite the absence of a clear class system, the idea of mixed government retained its beguiling appeal in America. It seemed an indispensable protection against tyranny and a reasonable rationalization for familiar colonial institutions. The governor's council, as it functioned in most colonies, seemed an approximation of a House of Lords. A few American royalists not only celebrated mixed government but even wanted to shape American society to fit it better. They proposed a titled nobility and an American episcopate as needed checks on popular factions. Even as sons of liberty bemoaned the excesses of prerogative in governor and council, royal governors in colonies such as Massachusetts, with an elected council, bemoaned the unchecked ascendancy of the democracy. Both sides acknowledged the need for class balance, and both charged the other with creating a fatal imbalance.

But not all colonial leaders subscribed to the orthodoxy of mixture. Thomas Paine, in his *Common Sense* pamphlets, launched the first brutal attack upon the British form of government and upon the idea of a mixed constitution. He ridiculed both monarch and lords, and recommended a simple, single as-

sembly with a revolving presidency. His proposals, so shock-
ingly naive to one like John Adams, won at least local support
and had a direct influence on the Pennsylvania constitution of
1776. But except for Franklin, few of the leaders of the revolutionary movement accepted Paine's heresy. Before the revolution, Cadwallader Colden of New York, a Tory politician and
noted scientist, supported mixture with much of the subtlety of
Harrington. John Randolph, Joseph Galloway, and John Dickinson all lauded it. Gouverneur Morris eloquently and almost
endlessly defended it as late as the convention of 1787.

Moderates were not alone in championing mixed government, although it had greater appeal to them than to the avowed
champions of the common people. Thomas Jefferson supported
the idea in his early, more coherent excursions into political
theory. His first two drafts of a proposed Virginia constitution
emphasized the bicameral principle as a requisite of balance. His
first draft even included a life-tenured senate, which he reduced
to nine-year terms in a second draft in order to keep alive the
idea that those who govern should return to the people. But he
still preferred life tenure to dependence on the people, since
popular choice was rarely distinguished by wisdom. After his
bitter experience as an almost helplessly weak governor in revolutionary Virginia, he used his famous *Notes on Virginia* to vent
his criticism of his state government. Among other things, he
condemned the Virginia Senate because it was homogeneous
with the House and thus unable to reflect the balancing influence of other interests and principles. Wealth and wisdom had
an equal voice in each house, nullifying all the benefits of separation. He also deplored the ineffective executive, who in most
areas remained at the mercy of the House.[4]

But it was John Adams who became the symbol of mixed
government. By 1780 he was probably the most determined defender of the principle in the whole world. He had not so clearly
supported mixed government as late as 1776, yet adopted the
idea wholesale in the struggles to achieve a constitution for Massachusetts. His three-volume *Defence of the Constitutions of Govern-*

ment of the United States, written in London in 1786–87, was above all a rambling defense of a balanced constitution and an unrelenting attack on all simple forms of government, particularly unchecked, one-assembly democracies. He avowedly wrote to refute the ideas of Turgot, but surely had an eye for developing events in the United States. His ponderous treatise, made up in large part of quotations, was the first significant work on the science of government produced by an American, and remains not only the most formalistic but one of the most provocative. In its analytic sections it possessed a breadth and a logical incisiveness absent in the *Federalist Papers,* the next and almost the only comparable early American contribution to theories of government.

Adams wrote before the Philadelphia Convention. Volume I arrived as the sessions opened, and may have influenced the deliberations slightly. In retrospect, his treatise seems a remarkably acute vindication of the convention's work, particularly the bicameralism and the strong executive. Adams avowedly wrote in defense of all the recent state constitutions, but in reality defended his own Massachusetts draft, which in turn shared more features with the federal Constitution than did that of any other state. As he completed his last volume, Adams was able to read the new federal Constitution and to proclaim the convention's work the "greatest single effort of national deliberation that the world has ever seen." Adams did not hide his admiration of the British constitution, but used all past history to prove the benefits of mixture. He examined all past republics, in Switzerland, in Italy, in ancient Greece. He showed the disasters that befell all simple constitutions, or such simple confederations as in Poland. He sought philosophic support all the way back to Homer. Given his limited time and limited research materials, it was a notable work of scholarship hastily glued together. The book hurt him politically. His use of conventional terms drawn from classical theory, his clear preference for monarchy over other simple forms, and his distaste for direct democratic assemblies all gained him the misleading label of "monarchist." [5]

Adams' defense of mixture came at the very time that a class-based politics seemed least appealing in America. Besides, ideas of functional separation had already confused the meaning of mixture and balance and helped create so much verbal confusion that any coherent thesis about government had small chance of acceptance.

The doctrine of separation of powers, as one final means of restricting government and avoiding tyranny, only developed in the seventeenth century. Its late origin is no accident. As early as Aristotle various men analyzed and named the varied functions of government. But no one tried to limit each function to a separate and distinct branch of government or to separate and distinct persons. Even today the idea of complete separation (of function, branch, and person) has elements of absurdity if projected as an ideal for an existing government, for at one point or another governmental powers meet and overlap. It is almost impossible to fit any real government into any functional schema, such as legislative, judicial, and executive. Only after some modern governments, and particularly the English, developed a degree of functional separation did anyone even perceive separation as a normative ideal.

In the Middle Ages even the most zealous enemies of absolutism assumed some form of limited monarchy. The king was, in the usual rhetoric, the chief magistrate. His duties embraced all recognized areas of government: the interpretation and enforcement of laws, including the highest judicial duties; diplomacy; the conduct of the military; and the appointment of inferior magistrates. If assemblies advised or shared power, they also participated in a wide range of governmental functions. Since, for much of the Middle Ages, law did not seem a product of government, only slowly did men conceive of a separate legislative role for princes or assemblies. The loosely used term of magistrate, at least through the seventeenth century, denoted deliber-

BALANCED SEPARATION / 154

ative, judicial, and executive functions without clear distinction. But, uncelebrated by any theory, a degree of specialization developed in modern governments of a mixed form. In England an independent judiciary became an ideal by the time of Sir Edward Coke. The successful claims of the two Houses of Parliament for a primary role in legislation finally made it possible to distinguish legislative and executive functions and, in part, assign them to different branches of government. Although the Houses of Parliament retained judicial authority, their legislative role was clearly distinct from the ongoing functions of government under the control of the king and his advisers or ministers. Some degree of functional specialization had become necessary even for efficiency. In the dislocations of the English revolutions, this separation seemed an important antidote for tyranny.[6]

In the aftermath of the Puritan Revolution, the temporary ascendancy of a single assembly not only destroyed the former mix of interests in government but also merged all governmental functions into one body. For some, the results seemed appalling. It was not discredited royalists but radical Levellers who first adopted separation as a principle of good government. John Lilburne challenged the members of the Long Parliament, who not only enacted laws but enforced them too, and also held profitable executive offices in the unbalanced system. There was no check on their power and no appeal from their decisions, for they also constituted the highest court of the realm. In petitions and proposed constitutions, the Levellers asked for separate legislative and executive branches (logically, they saw only two clear governmental roles—the making and the enforcing of laws). They wanted to be rid of placemen, or of nonlegislative roles for members of Parliament. But the Levellers hardly envisioned any absolute separation of powers. They appreciated some need for checks and balances, and thus areas of overlap. They even suggested judicial review by juries. Cromwell used two written constitutions (paternal grants, not popular compacts) to move back toward more mixture and more specialized functions. He reasserted executive powers and proposed an executive veto as a means of protecting that power against Parliament. The Restoration established even clearer boundaries between the king and the Houses of Parliament.[7]

Both Sidney and Harrington obliquely stressed advantages in separation, but they primarily emphasized the mixed form. Locke moved closer to an overt separation doctrine. He carefully distinguished three governmental functions: legislative, executive (including judicial), and federative (primarily foreign policy). Although he assumed the primacy of legislative power, he saw dangers in any complete merger of the legislature with the executive and federative head of the state, not the least being the intermittent nature of legislative deliberation. More crucial, if the frail men who made laws also enforced them, the temptation to exploit laws for private advantage would be overwhelming. In effect, then, after legislators met and enacted laws they should go home and, as private citizens, obey these same laws as enforced by permanent magistrates, even though, in an ultimate sense, those magistrates were inferior to, and dependent upon, the supreme legislative power.[8]

In eighteenth-century England a loose concept of separation remained at least a secondary ingredient of libertarian theory. The same opposition writers, the so-called Commonwealthmen or Whigs (the most ambiguous label in English political history), who provided so much of the rhetoric of the American Revolution, fought against what they saw as the corruption and subversion of the British constitution. Among other evils, John Trenchard condemned corrupt parliamentary placemen and deplored the members of Parliament who surrendered their independence for royal favors. But Trenchard always combined ideas of separation with more ancient ideas of balance. He wanted the king's ministers to be fully accountable to Parliament, a violation of perfect separation. Even as he urged separation of legislative and executive functions he asked for positive checks and points of overlapping jurisdiction, including impeachment powers for Parliament and a legislative veto by the king. Clearly, he feared any complete merger of powers and branches and wanted only a partial separation, valuing balance and independence more than isolation.[9]

Above all other writers, Montesquieu came to symbolize separation of powers. It is impossible to determine how much he influenced Americans. But his *Spirit of the Laws* (1748), one of the great treatises on politics and a book with a worldwide reputation, was an excellent authority for any American position. Thus, whenever possible, Americans appealed to the great Montesquieu much as they appealed to Locke. Montesquieu analyzed forms of government in his broad attempt to understand the varied sources of law. In several sections he particularly praised the British constitution, or at least an idealized version of it. He found in it an admirable separation of powers. For the first time he adopted the now conventional classification—legislative, executive, and judicial—and placed greatest emphasis upon the judiciary. This singling out of the judiciary alone made him appealing in America. Montesquieu clearly wanted different persons to exercise the different functions of government, and pointed to the tyranny in governments that merged all functions. Yet he never embraced an absolute form of separation and always blended ideas of separation with ideas of balance. He gave to the executive the power of convening the legislature and a veto over its enactments, and allowed the legislature restricted judicial roles and broad investigatory rights over the lower magistrates.[10]

Montesquieu at least appreciated the intricate relationship between separation and balance. Both were necessary for freedom under a government of laws. But when the two were in conflict, separation had to yield to checks and balances. The very checks that violate separation, such as an executive veto, are necessary to harmonize all interests. Nothing is gained by separating legislative, executive, and judicial functions in a government controlled by the aristocracy. A government dominated by the common people may adhere to separation and still impose a tyranny of the majority on minority interests. But once the proper mix or balance is secured, once government reflects consensus or concurrence in its legislature, then a degree of separation is a necessary but additive principle. At this level the concern is not an imbalance of interests but inescapable human frailty. Those who adopted extreme forms of separation always had an abiding distrust of government and of anyone or any group with a monopoly of power. To divide up the use of power was to restrain and tame it. If legislators passed laws looking to their own private aggrandizement, and they would surely do just that if they could get by with it, then executive offices, if separate and independent, could frustrate this power grab by ignoring such laws, even as the courts could nullify their effect by refusing enforcement. The mixed form was not a tool to restrain the power of government but to channel it in the paths of common interest. Separation was a tool to prevent a misuse of power and, very often, to prevent large accumulations of power.

A complete separation of powers, unlike a mixed constitution, is consistent with such simple forms of government as democracy and aristocracy. In fact, one has to escape the mix in order to have an absolute separation of function, branch, and person. All mixed constitutions provide internal checks and balancing mechanisms that cross any rigid lines of separation. It is at least conceivable, in a democracy, that a people could elect quite separate legislators, executives, and judges, allowing no overlap or mutual involvement among the three functions. If one branch exceeded its delegated powers, only the people could call it into account. Except in a very restricted geographical area, this system would pose difficulties, and to work at all would require very frequent elections or some recall mechanism. Such a pure form of separation invites instability. It achieves one possible goal—enough fragmentation that popular control is easier. It abets directly responsive forms of government, for it fosters a direct, rapid implementation of majority will and minimizes the possibility of a governmental elite with its own distinct interests.

Complete separation, unlike the mixed form, cannot cohere easily with legislative sovereignty. If a legislature, whether made up of one element or two or three, has ultimate power, appointing and holding responsible to itself the executive and the judges, it seems impossible for the two inferior branches to be either separate or independent. Thus, one practical implication of separation is a distinct and nondependent form of election or appointment for each branch of government. Only legislative appointment for life might escape the dependence, just as hereditary succession would bypass it. For these obvious reasons, the wide acceptance of separation reinforced ideas of popular sovereignty. Each part of government receives its power by consent of the people, however elected or appointed. In its most radical implications it supported democracy, or a government directly elected by, and immediately responsible to, the people. Thus, its political implications were quite divergent from those of mixed government. Mixture precluded any simple form, such as democracy, and almost always underwrote the idea of government by law. The mixing of classes and interests in legislation was in behalf of attaining truth or right reason as well as the greatest welfare of the whole society.

There was, in all these theories about governmental form, a possible third position. It never had a prominent defender until Madison and was part of no clear tradition. In fact, it was too much a hybrid and open to too many variations to have a coherent history. Briefly defined, it was the idea of checks and balances applied not to the classic forms of government but to the major branches and functions of government. Instead of completely separating them, why not let each check and frustrate the other in behalf of some form of internal equilibrium? Such ideas of balance existed not only in eighteenth-century theories of mixed government but also in most fashionable conceptions of nature, down to and including Franklin's ingenious theories about electricity. The idea was never more omnipresent. But as Madison realized, balance in government requires something other than complete separation. It is an active, functional principle, not a geometric one. The important attribute of each branch of government is not secure isolation but secure independence in its functioning. The best image is one of shifting lines of tension. If a legislature grabs for too much power, the executive branch fights back. It can only object if it has some positive check, such as a legislative veto. The courts need a protective power, such as judicial review. The legislature needs the right of impeachment to ward off an overzealous or corrupt executive. Such checks do not compromise the primary functional role of each branch.

This form of checks and balances, an almost thermostatic system of internal control, easily relates to other forms of balance in our governmental system. Perhaps this type of balancing justifies a two-house legislature. Even if both houses serve the same constituency, they slow and deepen the deliberative process; preclude hasty, whimsical, or hysterical action by one; and insure greater detachment and more critical rigor in legislation. The same types of internal balance could apply to overlapping or cooperative jurisdictions in executive departments.

Above all, the idea of checks and balances correlated with American federalism, or the *division of powers*. This federalism had Continental and classical precedents, well-developed theoretical support, and provocative precedents in the interplay between London and near autonomous colonial governments. But it also gained credence from ascendant ideas of separation and balance. Unlike mixed government, everyone realized that federalism was not a universal attribute of responsible government. It clearly fit only large commonwealths with developed local institutions. But, where applicable, it reflected one further means of checking power and avoiding tyranny. Thus, in America, as in no place else in the world, the idea of governmental balance would prevail. We would have governments that were mixed and balanced in form, separate and balanced in function, and divided and balanced in areas of jurisdiction.

8. Balanced Separation

The American Choice

THE PATTERN OF CONSTITUTIONAL DEVELOPMENT in America almost duplicated the historical evolution of doctrines about form. With the exception of Pennsylvania and Vermont, all the early state constitutions embodied the outward form of mixed government but very few adhered closely to its substance. Most state constitutions or declarations of right proclaimed the separation of powers, but no state achieved it. In subsequent revisions the states moved even closer to a purely formal mixture and achieved a greater degree of effective separation, but made these changes in behalf of forms of balance that cohered with neither traditional doctrine.

All the earliest state constitutions reflected the peculiar and temporary circumstances that led to their construction. With a few exceptions, such as Delaware, loyalists did not participate in the drafting. Thus, those Americans most likely to favor a strong executive were often excluded. The typical authors of constitutions, even in states that elected delegates to a separate convention, were former members of colonial assemblies, fresh from their climactic clashes with royal governors and loyalist councils, jealous of all prerogative power, and often willing to enhance their own political position. At least in 1776, the conventions had to proceed hastily and without much careful deliberation. Few of the first constitutions seemed to reflect any extensive airing of fundamental issues, although the surviving convention journals are all so cryptic and summary that we simply do not know very much about the clash of ideas. Finally, in eight states the conventions also served as interim governments, dividing their time unequally between constituent action and their necessary response to the overwhelming demands upon governments in a time of war and great confusion. Most conventions had to delegate drafting duties to committees, and then deliberate on only the more controversial sections.

The indelible memories of the recent past and the fear of prerogative help account for the most conspicuous shift from the colonial and British pattern—the severe erosion of executive power. At the outmost, it meant an overwhelming antipathy to hereditary monarchy. At first it also meant an intense fear of any arbitrary power, whoever exercised it. Americans would not have kings either in title or tenure or, for a time, even in power. This rejection was the most common justification for the label *republic*, which often meant little more than a government without a king at its head. But *republic* had far too many meanings, even in American usage, to serve as a precise label for the new constitutions. It variously symbolized a government with a large degree of popular participation, a nonarbitrary government of law above men, any government of mixed form (Adams), and even an equalitarian society without ranks and titles or artifice.

South Carolina in 1776 seemed an exception to this antimonarchical bias. It provided for an assembly-elected president with strong powers and an absolute legislative veto. But what the assembly could create it could break, and in its new, legislated constitution of 1778 it removed the veto power. The veto was not restored to the popularly elected governor provided for in South Carolina's enduring constitution of 1790. A few states went to the farthest extreme and practically eliminated the executive. From 1776 to 1784 New Hampshire had no governor, and Pennsylvania opted for a weak executive council with a revolving president. Virginia, North Carolina, Maryland, New Jersey, Georgia, and Delaware all provided for a governor who was almost a figurehead, to be elected by the legislature for brief terms, without veto powers, with few appointment privileges, and with severely restricted initiatives even in state administration. Such weak governors usually had to accept advice from some type of privy council, a direct carry-over from colonial governments. This bias against a strong executive was quite explicit and deeply entrenched. Except for Delaware, which shifted in 1789 to an elected governor with a modified veto (modified in the sense that the two houses could override it), these executive provisions remained in effect for an extended time—in Georgia until 1824, in Virginia until 1830, in North Carolina until 1835, in Maryland until 1837, and in New Jersey until 1844.[1]

This diminution of executive power of course violated all the established canons of a mixed constitution. The monarchical element, the balancing unity at the center of government, was completely missing. Without even a suspensive veto, these governors could not delay legislation in behalf of a broad consensus of interests. Legislative assemblies, and particularly lower houses, were practically sovereign.

A few states kept something closer to monarchical balance. Connecticut and Rhode Island kept the magisterial governor provided by their charters. New York did not complete its constitution until 1777, after the waning of the first, extreme reaction to former royal prerogatives. It provided for an elected governor with a share in both a modified veto and in major appointments (he presided over a review board and an appointments council). This new trend climaxed in Massachusetts in 1780 and in New Hampshire in 1784. John Adams, in drafting the Massachusetts constitution, merged Harrington's Oceana with the hallowed traditions of his state and region (one, perhaps whimsical, convention member moved to name the state Oceana). The constitution, as ratified, provided for a governor, elected for only one year, but with approximately the same powers as the royal governor had possessed before 1774. "His Excellency" was the head of state and commander-in-chief, had almost complete appointment powers, and could exercise a modified veto (again, two-thirds of the legislature could override). Eventually, this type of executive won acceptance in all the states, not so much because of the Massachusetts example or the appeal of ideas about mixed government but because of the pervasive influence of the federal Constitution of 1787.

Several states tried to insure that their governor be a man of wealth and stature. In 1778 South Carolina, at the upper extreme, required him to possess a freehold of 10,000 in British pounds; in Maryland the requirement was a 5,000-pound estate; in Georgia (1789) a 500-acre freehold plus 1,000 pounds in wealth; in Massachusetts a 1,000-pound freehold; and on down to a mere 500-pound estate in equalitarian New Hampshire. Age restrictions, when listed, ranged from a low of 25 in Maryland to 30 in other states. At least in this sense, the conventions wanted some of the dignity and stature formerly identified with a monarch or a royal governor. In 1776 it was not yet clear that most of the traditional federative functions (diplomacy, military) would accrue to the central government. Thus, whether he had much effective power or not, the governor was the symbolic head of state and needed the outward tokens of power. Had this type of figurehead governor survived in the states, the domestic executive roles might well have moved, by default, to legislative committees, and the United States might, for good or ill, have developed something close to a parliamentary form of government.

New York and Massachusetts set precedents not only with their strong executive but also in tying his strength to popular election. In this respect they joined the charter precedents in Connecticut and Rhode Island. Powerful as the Massachusetts governor was (John Adams modeled many features of the office on the British king), he still served for only one year (in New York for three). From John Adams' perspective, the power of the governor fulfilled the need for monarchical balance, while election to the office precluded gross incompetence or irresponsibility. The short term was a concession to New England tradition. Adams believed that popular and frequent elections worked well in Massachusetts, a relatively homogeneous state with a wide distribution of property, the restraints of piety, and the leaven of literacy, assets not present to as large an extent in other states or in the combined states. After experiencing the later pitfalls of party politics, old John Adams could even contemplate with sympathy a hereditary executive in America.[2]

Two class-based legislative assemblies were as crucial to a mixed government as was a balancing role for a strong chief magistrate. Again, in a purely formal sense, all the early states except Pennsylvania and Vermont seemed to meet this test. All were bicameral in form and all soon paid lip service to the idea of a senate representing age, wealth, and eminence (for a brief time in South Carolina [1776–1778], New Hampshire [1776–1784], and Georgia [1777–1789] the upper house was only a prefabricated creature of the lower, elected by it and from it). But after 1790 and Pennsylvania's second constitution, only Vermont held out against bicameralism, and even there the governor and his council exercised a suspensive veto.

The states adhered to the idea of some form of aristrocracy by either higher qualifications and longer terms for senators, or by a separate franchise for their election (a technique as rare as it was radical). South Carolina (in 1778 and 1790), Massachusetts, New Hampshire (1784), New Jersey, Maryland, North Carolina, Georgia (1789), and Delaware (1792) all had higher property qualifications (usually double, sometimes triple) for senators than for representatives. Most of these states, plus Pennsylvania (1790) and Virginia, had higher age requirements, longer terms, and some type of rotation in electoral lists. In an uncopied experiment, Georgia in 1789 required senators to be 38 years old, a sharp contrast to all others (25, 27, or 30). Only two states, North Carolina and New York, established two distinct (but not fully separate) constituencies (a strategy also written into the rejected Massachusetts constitution of 1778), and thus tried to make the senate the unique voice of wealth. In New York only freeholders with an estate of 100 English pounds could vote for senators; those with estates of 20 pounds, plus certain categories of tenants, could vote for the lower house. In North Carolina all taxpayers could vote for representatives, but only those with fifty-acre farms for senators. Maryland, in a unique effort to screen out men of refinement, wealth, and superior ability, permitted its regular electorate (those with thirty English pounds of wealth) to elect not senators but a college of senatorial electors.

These mild efforts to locate, empower, and benefit from, if not isolate, an American elite were not complete failures. Even to this day Americans probably expect greater maturity, wisdom, and political independence from senators, an assumed function of age and longer tenure and not of wealth or family status. Surely a detailed analysis of senators at the state and federal level in the early national period would reveal significant distinction in both wealth and eminence. But even in their origins the upper chambers hardly represented a distinct class, much less represented such a class exclusively. Both senators and representatives drew their support from property, for the generality of voters, even in states that allowed votes to nonfreeholders, owned land or commercial wealth. Men with secure wealth were the most likely to gain seats in both houses, not just in the one.

An aloof and prestigious upper house, as required by a mixed government, faced two almost fatal obstacles in the states—a deeply entrenched fear of any privileged aristocracy and the undermining effects of popular election. The very word *aristocrat* soon denoted not the exceptional ability and wisdom celebrated from Aristotle to Jefferson, or even the more prosaic ability to garner wealth and command other men as emphasized by Harrington and Adams, but rather special, deeply entrenched political privileges. The word suggested titles and arbitrary preferment. It had much of the color of *monarchy*, and created severe public-relations problems for exclusive orders such as the Society of Cincinnatus.

Adams sensed the difficulty of checking the power of wealth in an open society that would not recognize and dignify the wide disparities of wealth. In the absence of any formal aristocracy tied to families, he tried to dignify the governorship and the senate by high salaries and appropriate titles, making the positions so attractive, so flattering to the ego, that men of exceptional power and influence would be content to serve in these positions. Then they just might leave the democratic branch alone; in fact, that was necessary if there was to be a truly democratic house which accurately reflected the concerns and even the prejudices of the common people. If men of power could not find satisfaction in their own chamber, they would invade the local constituencies and the lower houses, using persuasion or economic leverage to influence votes in behalf of their special concerns, soon prostituting electoral politics to the machinations of large, even statewide, factions or parties. Clever men would thus seduce the people. Adams faced ridicule for his titles and condemnation for his monarchical and aristocratic heresies. Even today few people are willing to face the hard logic of his central assumptions: wealth is the prime source of political power in America; a few men with great wealth can rule over many men with small wealth; the highest achievable hope for a free society is to maintain the power of the few in equal balance with that of the many (in all history a goal never achieved for very long).

Popular election for limited terms is simply not consistent with an aristocracy of the type envisioned in a mixed constitution. Adams came to appreciate this fact and speculated about the advantages of appointment or election for life. The more optimistic advocates of direct, representative government, including Jefferson in a few of his more hopeful moments, expected elections to serve as effective screening devices. The people would surely turn to their more talented men for governmental service. Adams knew better. Besides, he did not want the

masses in their local constituency to select aristocrats to represent them in their own chamber, for such men would not really
look out for the interests of the masses, although they might be
clever enough to persuade the majority that they did just that.
In large senatorial districts the people were most likely to turn
to their more charismatic and powerful superiors (possibly passing over more reserved men of superior talents and virtues), but
even then the electoral process distorted the proper role of senators. Drawing their power directly from the people, they had to
please the people. Wealthy senators either had to turn their
backs on the interests of their own class or employ the more
likely expedient of covert strategies to serve their own interests
while indulging in enough demagoguery to make the people
willing accomplices. Unless tied to small local districts, unsul-
lied by the interventions of the wealthy and unpolluted by parties, the lower house could suffer the same fate. When chosen
by the same constituents, it was likely that the two houses
would attract men of the same calibre. Both would be under
obligation to bow before the same icons of representative democracy. If popular election did not assure this dependence, the
subsequent two-party system did.

In such an analysis Adams was prophetic. He did not describe the intentions of the early conventions. We know too little
about their deliberations to assess their exact desires, but one
can easily guess that the bicameral form more nearly reflected a
recourse to accustomed forms than any self-conscious attempt to
implement a doctrinaire version of mixed government. Adams
also seemed to assume certain ideas about representation. With
his usual honesty, he sincerely applauded annual elections, and
always wanted them at least for the democratic branch. But his
version of mixed government really required two forms of representation, a distinction he never made. One clue to contrasting
forms of representation, and to certain lingering ambivalences in
American government even in the present, lurked in the Puritan
heritage in Massachusetts.

In Calvinist political theory, as still preached in election ser-

mons as late as 1780, the sovereign people had one morally necessary political role—to choose their own form of government
within the limits of natural law. Since, in actual fact, the people
of Massachusetts chose a mixed form, with all branches elective,
they served a second continuing role—voting. But what did voting mean? In the older Calvinist perspective it was merely a
mode of selecting independent magistrates, not a tool for direct
popular control over government. The magistrate had his authority from God and governed according to established law and
the prompting of conscience, not according to popular desires.
He had to look out for the real interests of his constituents and
of the whole society. The people had a moral and religious
obligation to respect and obey such a magistrate, whether they
agreed with him or not. But quite clearly the people of Massachusetts did not accede to such a limited electoral role. There,
and in other Puritan colonies, the record is a very complex one,
of resentful and jealous towns carefully instructing their delegates to the General Court, even in the midst of a brief, one-
year term, and holding them to a strict accountability at election
time. On the other hand, elected magistrates at all levels, in a
tradition that began with Winthrop and had full support from
the clergy, often lectured constituents on their duties and obligations and insisted upon their independence of local opinion. In
effect, representation in Massachusetts became a dialogistic af-
fair, a complex interaction between the people and their "representatives." The same role tension developed in the churches of
New England. The elected minister, in good conscience, had to
speak the truth to his congregation, and had to convince them
that they must respect the authority of his position enough to
listen even when they disagreed. In fact, they did not always listen to what they did not want to hear and often used the threat
of expulsion as a method of censorship. It is hard to document
such an assertion, but it seems that both magisterial and minis-
terial leeway shrunk with each passing generation. But as late as
the Revolution both ministers and magistrates could still appeal
to the dignity and independence of their special calling. John

Adams as president beautifully illustrated the special virtues and political liabilities of a Calvinist magistrate.

By 1780 the magisterial image hardly fit the delegates to lower houses in New England, and only slightly better fit the "gentlemen" who dominated lower assemblies in the South. John Winthrop's fear of a directly responsive government, of an awful democracy, was realized in the development of the lower houses. John Adams welcomed the shift. By his theory of mixed government, it was entirely proper that a dialogistic form of representation prevail in the democracy. He wanted a delegate from a small unified district to reflect his constituency, not excel it. He should remain in close contact with local opinion, but not suspend all private judgment or move only by the guidance of opinion surveys. Adams simply assumed that, on most issues, the delegate would be so similar to his constituents that he could act in good conscience and yet do just what they wanted. In the democratic branch, election would and should lead not only to a responsive and obliging agent but also to a representative in the most literal sense—a copy of his constituency.

After the American Revolution the magisterial image really applied only to judges. Safe from electoral politics and generally enjoying the long-sought goal of life tenure, they symbolized a still-revered system of law and were in no direct sense dependent upon popular opinion. They even retained much of the dignity of old, and had the charge of upholding, or in some sense "representing," the long-term interests of the community. But in order to uphold the idea of mixture, the governor and the senators also needed some of this magisterial distance. Any mixed government needed senators with greater literacy, governmental experience, and leadership talents—the very characteristics that usually correlate with wealth and social standing—than did members of a lower house. Thus, the insoluble dilemma: the people elected a senate that, to play its proper role, had to turn away from the people. It had to protect large property, preserve order, and resist popular enthusiasms.

The prestige of mixed theories helped create bicameralism in

America, but a purely formal arrangement could not undo social realities. Almost as soon as it was formally achieved, mixed government lost almost all its meaning and soon had few supporters. The sovereign people not only chose their form of government but soon demanded control over government. Adams always affirmed popular sovereignty (no one understood its logic better), but he tried to persuade the states that they should not set up a simple democracy, that they should in wisdom choose a mixed or republican form. But it was unrealistic to expect the people who elected senators and governors to view them in a completely different light than their representatives in lower houses. They accepted longer terms, slightly different roles, and special qualifications for senators. Prevailing patterns of deference made it likely that they would elect their "betters" to both houses. But they still wanted elected officials to represent their interests as they perceived them. After all, is that not what elections are all about? And it would have taken a better preacher than even John Adams to persuade them that they were wrong, that in pushing their distorted claims of popular sovereignty they were really building an unbalanced democracy which, despite their best intentions, would not check the ascendancy of an oligarchy but all too quickly allow it to use its virtually unlimited economic and political power to dominate the masses, using the heady and beguiling flattery of votes as a tool of co-optation. When the oligarchs controlled two branches of government, only the judges would remain as protectors of the real interests of the people or of the whole community, and they would often lack the power to effect their decisions.

As all the other states struggled with problems of mixture, Pennsylvania unsuccessfully tried to follow a different drummer. In the midst of a considerable shift of political power, its equalitarian convention approved a unicameral legislature and condemned all vestiges of aristocracy. The new constitution immediately became a center of controversy in a sharply divided state. The controversy produced the largest volume of polemics on governmental form so far produced in America. The foes of the constitution included most of the "best" and most propertied citizens of the state. They called themselves "republicans" and used every means possible to embarrass the existing Assembly, which they described as mob government under an execrable form of democracy. Early critics, including Benjamin Rush, took the mixed form as gospel, and thus indicted the lack of any aristocratic branch. Much as Adams did later, Rush worried about the rich dominating the yeomen. Others worried about the dominance of barbarians and the exclusion of the most able and talented men of the state. But even early the anticonstitutionalists did not dare challenge the intense popular antipathy to any privileged elite. Thus, they continued to lambast the dangers of unchecked legislative power and to appeal to the need for restraints on concentrated power, but without suggesting any need for the class balance implied by the mixed theory.[3]

The unique Pennsylvania Council of Censors met in 1783–84 to search out defects in and violations of the Pennsylvania constitution. By a narrow margin, the anticonstitutionalists dominated the council and proceeded to declare the constitution defective in all ways. The unicameral system prevented any effective checks upon governmental power or upon the dominance of prevailing factions, allowed the Assembly to usurp executive and judicial functions, and suffered from the weakness of the compound executive. The majority drafted a number of amendments which would have created a two-house legislature, a single, elected, and powerful governor with veto powers, and independent and life-tenured judges—or a constitution close to that of Massachusetts. A large minority of "constitutionalists" issued a minority report and effectively blocked any submission of amendments. The majority had to be content with a long detailed list of specific violations of the existing constitution by a power-grabbing assembly. The published work of the council had significance well beyond Pennsylvania. It helped cement the general view that Pennsylvania's experiment in unicameralism was a complete failure, and gave powerful ammunition to those who desired a separation of powers. The council never met again. In 1789, a year before its scheduled reconstitution, the assembly itself, under anticonstitutional dominance, called a new convention which, in 1790, ended the infamous experiment by a fully orthodox constitution with a bicameral legislature.[4]

There was no clear clash of argument in the council. The friends of the constitution rejected the mixed idea as a concealed technique for reviving a hierarchical society, with a few men dominating the state government. Instead of a bicameral system safely isolating aristocrats, as Rush had argued earlier, they believed it was a form which created and maintained special privilege. They did not accept Adams' contention that an aristocracy is inevitable in a free society; they saw it as an unwanted, artificial creation. The anticonstitutionalists did not counter these arguments. Instead, they appealed to another popular fear—an uncontrolled and arbitrary government. The need was for effective checks against one dominant branch of government. Thus they emphasized not class balance but a form of separation with internal checks and balances. In Pennsylvania this argument was more beguiling than any open defense of an "upper" house. Relying on fears of governmental aggrandizement, the anticonstitutionalists successfully solicited popular support in their effort to bring government to heel.[5]

In Pennsylvania the defense of bicameralism became an adjunct to a modified doctrine of separation. This shift of emphasis was prophetic. From 1776 on the separation of powers was almost a verbal truism while mixed ideas lost favor and relevance. Virginia, Maryland, North Carolina, Georgia, Massachusetts, and New Hampshire (1784) all included a specific separation clause in their declarations or constitutions. Pennsylvania and Delaware very carefully defined the distinct branches of government. The Maryland wording was the most direct and simple: "That the legislative, executive and judicial powers of government, ought to be forever separate and distinct from each other." This separation clause carried by only one vote, but the close passage probably reflected not sizeable opposition but delegate support for an even stronger wording just rejected in the form of an amendment. In Massachusetts John Adams realized that a mixed form, which required internal checks, was not consistent with a complete separation of powers. In his draft of a declaration of rights he included two elaborate clauses to protect judicial independence. The convention deleted them and substituted the standard separation clause, which it approved by voice vote and which the towns ratified. Whatever the doctrine meant, it had a broad appeal.[6]

But why, historians still ask, did the states so readily affirm separation as a principle and then betray it in practice? The universally weak executive in early constitutions and the extensive appointive and elective powers in the legislatures seem to document such a betrayal. The convention delegates undoubtedly did not so perceive their work. States such as Virginia, in their determination to end all arbitrary prerogative, wanted a separate but also a quite weak executive. The conflict between these two purposes only became evident in time. Technically, all the states did provide for a separation of function. Except in Pennsylvania, the life tenure of judges largely nullified their dependence on the appointing legislature. But because of legislative election or appointment the limited-term governors were almost helplessly dependent. Given the existing priorities, there was no easy way out of this dilemma. Later, the popular election of governors with areas of autonomous power eliminated this most obvious source of functional interference. But in 1776 the states did not want to create a powerful executive with his own electoral constituency and a broad leeway in operating the government. The great danger of tyranny then seemed to lurk not in intermittent assemblies but in self-serving and permanent executive agencies. The image of king and ministers, or royal governors and councils, remained dominant.

Surprisingly, the early state constitutions came as close to a functional separation of powers as did any later ones. What they did not achieve was functional independence, a concept rarely grasped or appreciated in 1776. In effect, independence required a near equality of power in each of the three branches and also internal checks and balances, or marginal areas of interaction and overlap, and thus something far less than absolute separation. Massachusetts set the enduring precedent, although not by design. It was simply a by-product of the mixed ideal which Adams wrote into his draft. The mixture required not only bicameralism (irrelevant to separation) but also the monarchical element; hence the executive veto, and also an efficient, powerful executive to activate the laws that would emerge from the concurrence of interests in the complex legislature. As Adams conceived it, a government had to be able to act expeditiously. In many contexts the scope of government should be very broad; within the limits of justice a government might have to govern a great deal. He wanted a governor with broad appointive and federative powers. But the other branches were also powerful; the two legislative assemblies not only initiated all legislation but had impeachment powers to keep the governor honest. The securely independent courts also had a defensive weapon in their right to disallow legislation on constitutional grounds.

Massachusetts achieved what the anticonstitutionalists in Pennsylvania idealized—a balanced but only partial separation of powers. In the legislature the varied terms and qualifications of senators insured a bare remnant of upper-class distinction, but largely the balance depended upon the fact of separation rather than a difference of class and constituency. It was, in practice, more an instrument of caution and prudence than of fundamental concurrence. To a large extent the three branches of government remained separate, but not so separate as to be defenseless against the imperial grabs of another branch. The internal checks assured a degree of equilibrium, or what the early state governments so obviously lacked. This qualified separation and complete independence, when accepted in other states and at the national level, meant that America could never develop a parliamentary system like the British. Separation precluded any formal merging of legislative and executive branches. But, not being a rigid form of separation, it not only allowed but

justified later legislative initiatives by executives as well as extensive legislative scrutiny of executive performance. It also gave
support to the strong form of judicial review that American
courts finally won within the balanced system. These internal
checks seemed necessary to restrain government, in its entirety,
to the specific trust granted it by a people in a constitution.

Contrary to later criticism, this type of balanced separation
did not of necessity frustrate government or render it impotent
in times of crisis. It did not even require the collaborative cata-
lyst of a two-party system in order to work. Of course it sty-
mied governmental initiatives when there was no clear popular
mandate for action, but this area was the very one where, in
eighteenth-century belief, a government should be impotent.
Even without the clear class harmony desired by advocates of
mixed government, the American version of bicameralism and
executive veto did make the legislative process so complex that
varied minority constituencies had different avenues for block-
ing legislation, or at least slowing its progress. In that sense the
balanced separation usually required for expedient legislation
something considerably more than a mere numerical majority (of
votes or of concentrated power) and something closer to a concurrence between a majority and large minorities. But, given
such a concurrence, which seemed in all ways desirable on critical legislative issues, the legislature could act with dispatch.

Perhaps more important, a balanced separation allowed the
executive, in part because of his independence of the legislature,
to act with great efficiency in all areas in which the very security
of a republic depended upon speed and efficiency. Much more
than in a parliamentary system the executive in American governments became a temporary monarch. But he had much less
power than did prime ministers to coordinate executive goals
with the legislature, and to the extent that he could do so he had
to depend upon a chance convergence of parties or upon an effective appeal to the public (eventualities not anticipated by the
early conventions). The exact leeway for executive action, of
course, was always a compactual issue—how much power did

the people want him to have. Massachusetts and the federal Constitution illustrated that it could be a great deal, even as Virginia illustrated that it could be very little. The point is that separation did not, in itself, require either a checkmated legislature or an impotent executive. When separation joined with independence it even opened up new possibilities for executive action. Under the formal arrangements accepted by Americans, they could have about as much government as they desired. The seeming impotence of early governments was not as much a function of form as of choice. But the balanced separation, unlike an unlimited monarch or a simple, unchecked majoritarian democracy (to cite two forms of absolutism), was quite congenial to their usual choice of very limited government.

The federal Constitution, in large part because of purely extraneous reasons or as a result of doctrinal compromises, almost perfectly reflected a maturing American version of balanced separation. Subsequently, the federal form had a decisive influence upon revised state constitutions. By the mid-nineteenth century the typical state constitution was as similar in form to the federal as the dome on its state capitol was to the one in Washington. The federal convention invited a wide-ranging debate on government, as did the state controversies over ratification. In Philadelphia all the classic arguments for both mixture and separation had able spokesmen, but in the end neither prevailed in pure form. More brilliantly than anyone else, James Madison defended the hybrid product.

The form of a new federal government was secondary to the most critical issue at Philadelphia and in the ratifying conventions—the power of such a government. The crucial debate concerned the need for a new government and the relative powers and divergent roles of the state and federal governments. The prevailing majority at Philadelphia wanted, and believed they secured, a constitution that created a federal government strong enough and stable enough to provide a needed protection for national interests and for rights of property, the most critical and most threatened of human rights. They tried to set up a center of power no longer under the control of state governments, and what they saw as ascendant and often whimsical, irresponsible, and excessively equalitarian popular majorities at the state level. Frightening paper-money issues, foreign policy embarrassments, and the type of public disorder illustrated by Shays's Rebellion, however exaggerated and distorted, provided the backdrop and the excuse for a stronger national government. Much more than anyone might have predicted, the proposed federal Constitution either imitated such state constitutions as those of Massachusetts or New Hampshire, or was at the leading edge of constitutional revision. It came as close as possible to an emerging majority view on the best form for a "republican" government.

John Adams ascribed preternatural wisdom to the convention because it seemed to him that it wisely incorporated his own theory of mixture. Perhaps Gouverneur Morris saw in it the direct influence of his persuasive arguments to the same end, but both men erred in their causal judgments. The main outward evidence of mixture—the bicameral Congress and the strong executive—scarcely embodied any coherent theory. The executive fulfilled the desire for an effective national government, particularly in foreign policy, pushed by the nationalists. As every schoolchild knows, the bicameralism provided a happy answer to the competition between large and small states. But, at the very least, the delegates dutifully listened to Morris' lengthy speeches on the hallowed principles of mixture and made him happy by their handiwork.

At the convention, Morris defended mixture in language even more pungent than Adams'. He believed the democratic branch of government needed the check by aggrandizing aristocrats in behalf of safety and secure property. Both the common people and the aristocrats have abilities and virtues; both have appropriate vices. They balance nicely. The Senate should represent property and an autocratic spirit, or great pride and a compelling desire to lord it over others. Of course, the Senate would do wrong. Morris hoped it would, for only then could its excesses check those of the democracy. The rich would try to establish dominion and enslave everyone else. They always had and they always would. The only protection was isolation in a separate body representing their separate interests. Without such isolation they would become an oligarchy, and a vulgar commercial one at that (much more than did Adams, Morris envisioned an aristocracy of merchants and bankers and not large landowners). If the democracy prevailed, it would lay siege to property and fall into anarchy. To preserve the balance between the two groups, Morris desired a strong executive. But he emphasized that a strong president, representing all the people, would not so much check the power of either main interest group as frustrate the normal tendency of legislatures to dominate government. In this way he capped his defense of mixture with a modified doctrine of separation and functional balance.[7]

Other delegates at Philadelphia repeated some of Morris' arguments, but no one made mixture such an orthodoxy. The libertarian and antidemocratic views of a majority of delegates made some aspects of mixture very appealing. John Dickinson wanted senators to be elected by their state legislatures, not only because this method would favor small states (his most basic concern) but also to get distinguished legislators, high in social rank and in property—as close to an American House of Lords as possible. He even referred to such a group as an American nobility. Elbridge Gerry condemned popularly elected senators because they would represent landed property. Election by more aristocratic state legislatures would favor commercial interests. Thus, with Morris, he envisioned a new form of class balance—agriculture versus commerce and banking. John Randolph saw the role of the second branch as control over democratic impulse. Hamilton, in an almost whimsical airing of his extreme views, asked for election of senators for life. Others favored a senate without reference to mixture. James Wilson, the archnationalist, wanted a popularly elected senate to prevent legislative despotism. Roger Sherman, in a very practical argument, said two houses were justified in behalf of more wisdom and ability in government; the important concern was that senators be more able than representatives. Charles Pinckney of South Carolina denied any classical orders or estates in America, or any equivalent for either a nobility or a monarchy. As a society with universal property ownership, America had no dangerous rich who needed to be isolated and checked. He saw the Senate as a needed balance between executive prerogative and the power of the people.[8]

Madison devoted five of *The Federalist Papers* (nos. 62–66) to a defense of bicameralism and, in particular, the Senate. He saw a state-elected Senate as a bridge between the federal government and the states as well as a salutary check on the lower house. Much of his criticism of a single house resembled John Adams'. Using historical as well as logical arguments, he contended that a single house would be fickle and unstable, ready to fall into the hands of a moneyed and enterprising few. It would lack legislative expertise, foresight, and a long-range sense of responsibility. But he never suggested that the corrective was an American aristocracy, drawn from an elite constituency, although he appreciated the advantages of indirect election (the one, important feature of the federal Senate that distinguished it from upper houses in the states and, until a two-party system virtually nullified the effect, brought it a bit closer to the principles of mixture). Rather than status, Madison emphasized age and length of term, and thus the prospect of more stable character and less impulsive legislation as well as a competent advisory role in several executive areas (appointment, treaties). He confidently predicted the normal superiority of the House, not simply because it originated money bills but because its mode of apportionment made it the special instrument of large states. To say the least, his was a truncated version of the mixed doctrine, but probably the only version that still had wide popular appeal.[9]

The strong federal executive, even less than the Senate, reflected doctrinal imperatives. The president, as the nationalists conceived his proper function, would exercise the federative role for the whole country, both as commander-in-chief and as head of our diplomatic corps. His legislative veto protected his power and more nearly reflected a separation doctrine than any desire for a balancing unity in a mixed constitution. Only John F. Mercer of Maryland defended executive power as a means of restraining the power of an aristocracy and protecting the country against a plundering legislature dominated by men of wealth and ability.[10]

The most troublesome issue was not the power of the president but his mode of election. Nationalists wanted, above all, to bypass state legislatures. The developed doctrine of separation as well as widely aired criticisms of the early state governments worked against election by the federal Congress. But James Wilson was in a minority in preferring the seeming alternative—popular election. The classic image of a monarch lived on. The delegates desired a president above all partisan politics. His required talents had little to do with popularity. There seemed no likelihood that the people would always choose well, and the very electoral process invited political factions or parties, which almost everyone deplored. The electoral college, borrowed directly from Maryland, or more distantly from the Papacy or the Holy Roman Empire, was a happy compromise. It either elected the president or limited the choices open to the House of Representatives. This means of election largely rested presidential power in the people and not in state governments—a nationalist victory. But at least the distribution of electoral votes and the rules for House election favored the smaller states, while the local election of members of a deliberative college seemed to avoid all the pitfalls of direct democracy or the vulgarity of avowed candidates competing for the highest office of the land. The indirect mode of election for both the president and the Senate and the appointment of judges seemed to confine electoral politics to manageable local districts, where democracy worked best and in which outside factions or demagogues had minimal leverage. In this sense the Constitution rather elaborately protected the people and their liberties from all the obvious dangers of democratic politics spread over a vast geographic region, yet in no sense limited their ultimate sovereignty.

The variance of views toward mixed government did not carry over to the idea of separation. No delegate spoke out against it in principle, although it was largely irrelevant to the few defenders of the old confederation of sovereign states. They did not envision but nevertheless feared extended, independent executive and judicial functions at the federal level, and by their state-rights advocacy opposed the balanced separation so ably espoused by Madison and so much a part of the nationalist position. In behalf of the fullest possible harmony of the whole system, Madison struggled unsuccessfully for a federal congressional veto over conflicting state legislation (an anticipation of the role eventually assumed by the federal courts under the Fourteenth Amendment).[11]

The formal deficiency of the completed Constitution, for some critics, was just the absence of separation of branches and powers. The president shared in legislation. The vice president presided over the Senate. Congress constituted courts and served as an impeachment body. The Senate concurred in major appointments and in treaties. The president and the Senate appointed federal judges. The convention delegates were quite aware of this blending, and offered arguments for each particular case. Madison agreed with almost everyone else that liberty depended upon some degree of separation, at least to the extent that one branch could not take over the work of another or two branches combine against the third. But, as he saw it, independence was fully as critical as separation. He joined with Wilson and Morris in defending the functional overlap necessary to protect the integrity of each, or in behalf of what Morris called a "protected" separation.[12]

In *The Federalist Papers* (47–51), Madison gave the most detailed defense yet penned of a modified separation of functions, a secure independence for each branch, and a continuing harmony between the parts. He expanded upon the arguments of

Pennsylvania anticonstitutionalists, whom he read and quoted extensively. He accepted, perhaps too uncritically, the widely accepted critique of both the unicameral system in Pennsylvania and the weak and dependent executives in fully half the states. The problem, as he saw it, was to keep all branches of government honest and at their appointed tasks. He believed that complete separation, as expressed on paper, required continuous constitutional action by a people in order to keep each branch in its proper place. Apart from its impracticality, this continuous intervention would work in the favor of the legislative branch, which alone could take its case back to the people. It would also soon strip government of the veneration necessary for stability, and too frequently subject grave constitutional issues to the passions of the people, cheapening and eroding the great sanctity that should attach to compacts of government. Complete separation also precluded appointment of one branch by another, as with judges under the federal system. It would mean across-the-board elections of all officials, which threatened the level of competence and technical skill needed in such areas as the courts. Thus, the only workable solution, and one quite consistent, he argued, with a proper understanding of Montesquieu, were the internal checks or defensive mechanism of the federal Constitution. Finally, bicameralism was only an extension of this principle to the one branch, in America at least, most likely to exceed its allocated powers. Two houses, in a sense, represented a balancing mechanism in a balancing mechanism.[13]

Madison's case was a bit too retrospective and adhered too closely to all the particular details of the object of his advocacy to be fully convincing as a theoretical exercise. His contrived examples allowed both exceptions and counterexamples. His whole analysis rested upon challengeable assumptions about America—its plurality of interests, its lack of a distinct aristocracy—and upon assumptions of universality that really reflected only the peculiarities of time and place. But no matter. His retrospective rationalization of the handiwork of the convention (he never argued that the convention set out, self-consciously and prophetically, to develop such a near perfect mechanism) remains a far more accurate commentary on government forms in America than the more traditional formalism of Adams or the more abstract guidelines of Montesquieu.

The final act in the constitutional drama occurred in the state ratifying conventions, and particularly in the more divided and close contests. The delegates who signed the Constitution in Philadelphia usually led the defense at the state level. Only Alexander Hamilton in New York and James Wilson in Pennsylvania attained a level of generality that rivaled *The Federalist Papers*. The state debates rarely focused specifically on governmental form. The overriding issue was always power, or the widely expressed fears of a fully consolidated and distant federal government with excessive powers and inadequate safeguards for individual liberty or state sovereignty. The absence of a bill of rights, the extensive taxing powers, and a degree of federal control over the militia best engaged the issue of power, and not the relative powers of the individual branches or their degree of separation.

Mixed ideas had small impact. James Wilson generally defended a mixed model but only the youthful Charles Pinckney of South Carolina used the full spectrum of historical arguments. Even he hedged a bit, insisting that the Senate would provide the wisdom and experience of an aristocracy without being an aristocracy. The House came in for more criticism than the Senate, either because of its biennial election (New Englanders still believed that annual election was a needed safeguard) or the seemingly small number of representatives. Only New York delegates made the power of the Senate a key issue. As a whole, the status of the Senate as the unique representative of the individual states disarmed critics. Ironically, the only extended argument in favor of a more independent Senate came from an avowed democrat, and the most vitriolic critic of the new Constitution, Patrick Henry of Virginia. His shotgun attack had only one clear focus—to protect the vulnerable liberties of the people of Virginia against federal usurpation. From this perspective, he argued that the British form of government, with a life-tenured House of Lords, contained a far better checking device than a new federal government in which all branches drew their power from the people.[14]

The Constitution also fared well on the issue of separation. In Pennsylvania, James Wilson was defensive about the areas of overlap between the branches, but still stressed that the completed Constitution required more separation than existed in any national government in the world. Madison played a crucial but subdued role in the Virginia debates, and did not expand upon his *Federalist* defense of balanced separation. James Iredell used all of Madison's arguments in a futile attempt to win ratification in North Carolina. In New York Melancton Smith, who debated Hamilton on the relative merits of aristocracy and democracy, made inadequate separation one minor argument in his detailed criticism of the various inducements to an American elite.[15]

Most of the state debates hinged on very insecure estimates about the future. By the advantage of hindsight, many of the fears of the opponents, as they sought out every possible ambiguity of language, every possible indication of some conspiracy against liberty, every loophole that might allow future officials to aggrandize themselves, now seem ridiculously exaggerated or almost paranoid. But opponents were often no more mistaken in their expectations than the defenders who, above all else, never anticipated the early development of a party system and a fundamental transformation of the meanings and operations of so much of their handiwork. Thus, the one all-important question in 1788 could not be answered with any assurance by either side in the debate. Would the new federal government protect and enhance life, liberty, and property in their most lofty moral connotations? And, within these imperatives, would it, could it, remain a willing servant of its legitimate but often divided and confused master—the American people?

Epilogue

B Y AT LEAST ONE TEST, Americans did well in designing their governments. They have endured. Despite a few examples of alternative traditions (such as the positive law in Louisiana) or significant constitutional experiments (like Nebraska's unicameralism) or attempts to convert balanced government into a type of direct democracy (in such devices as initiative referendum, and recall) the early forms have encountered few successful challenges. But major changes in the society and in the actual functioning of our institutions have confounded some of the expectations of the founders. These changes deserve attention.

At least on the surface, the principle of popular sovereignty has seemed most invulnerable to the erosions of time. Our covenants still rest on either popular consent or popular neglect, and in most jurisdictions remain open to easy amendment and revision. Except for some very recent threats to the right of travel, we still permit the only possible relief for those individuals who cannot win support for their beliefs and who cannot give even tacit consent to our basic institutions as they now function— they may freely emigrate to other countries and take with them all their possessions. With time, the distinction between constitutional and legislative process has often blurred. Particularly in the states, and increasingly at the federal level, constitutional amendments have served as means of bypassing the legislature or overcoming a political impasse. Thus voters, in approving more and more constitutional amendments, in reality legislate rather than set the limits or provide the enabling authority for representative bodies. This distortion of constitutional process seemingly abets a form of direct, majoritarian democracy, with all the implied threats for minorities. In actual fact, it often abets small, privileged minorities who take advantage of the lack of informed discussion and debate on often complex and technical constitutional issues and of the small number of votes actually cast.

The welfare and happiness of individuals is still the avowed purpose of our governments. In fact, I doubt that Americans have ever been more conscious of rights than in the present, and in many areas governments have never provided as many protections—mostly in criminal procedures, religion, and private expression. But the now celebrated rights of self-expression have a quite different import in the present than in the past. Formally much broader, they are effectively much more restricted. When the only forum for verbal persuasion was the village lectern or the local newspaper, whatever freedom of expression existed was at least open to the ordinary individual. Today, when opinion is largely shaped by national media, an effective platform is available only to the affluent or to those who speak for massive interest groups. Access to the soapbox is now an almost empty privilege. At the same time, national informational networks, electronic surveillance, and increased governmental scrutiny of citizens all threaten the privacy that many people associate with free expression.

Even as Americans framed their first constitutions they were already expanding the spectrum of sacred rights to include the vote. Popular sovereignty, rigorously interpreted, gave every male a rightful voice in forming a government. The right of property seemed to require some form of participation for all taxpayers, since only they could approve taxes. The revolutionary arguments over vicarious representation only reinforced existing American suspicions of any but an actual, direct form of geographical representation. Thus, there was no effective opposition to elective legislatures. The remaining area of contention was the franchise. Who should vote? The colonial pattern prevailed in most early constitutions—voting rights either for freeholders (or equivalents for city dwellers) or for men with a specified amount of wealth. These requirements excluded many taxpayers and men of recognized ability. But the states rarely enforced all franchise rules and in many local areas almost anyone who wanted to badly enough could vote. Besides, the high qualifications eroded very quickly in most states, and usually without any concerted effort by nonvoters. From the beginning, Pennsylvania and North Carolina (for its lower house) allowed all white male taxpayers to vote. Kentucky and Tennessee entered the union with universal white manhood suffrage. Freehold or large wealth requirements fell in Georgia in 1789, in Delaware in 1792, in Maryland and South Carolina in 1810, in Connecticut in 1818, in New York in 1821, and in Massachusetts in 1822. Only in clearly laggard states, particularly Virginia (1830) and Rhode Island (1842), did the franchise become a fervent political issue. By 1854, when North Carolina abolished its freehold requirements for senatorial elections, some form of taxation (often what amounted to a poll tax) remained the only widespread impediment to voting for adult, white males. By then most any American would have listed the right to vote along with hallowed procedural protections and expressive freedoms.

The achieved right to vote paralleled a growing penchant of Americans to describe their political system as "democratic" or as a "democracy." The varying uses of the word *democracy*, the diverse images and values associated with it, make up a fascinating story in our history, and one too rarely noted. In the revolutionary and early national periods the word already had a heavy symbolism. A few precise theorists, such as John Adams, still used the word pejoratively to describe a system in which the people, or massed majorities of them, ruled directly, unchecked by truth, by right, or by law. It thus denoted one form of absolutism. For Alexander Hamilton the word suggested something close to mob rule. But even by the ratification debates, the word generally had a positive association and some polemical value. All sides appealed to *democracy*, both in defending and criticizing the new constitution.

In its positive meanings, *democracy* became a loose synonym for popular sovereignty and for direct representation. Those who acclaimed the word at the very least referred to a government founded in popular consent and open to some continuous popular control. Avowed democrats still disagreed on the controverted issues, such as the correct basis of the franchise or the status of an upper house. In America the word *democracy* rarely suggested the radical views of a Thomas Paine or any widespread desire to abolish either internal checks on the popular will or nonrepresentative branches like the courts. In inexact, popular celebration the word soon blended the idea of limiting authority and assured freedom (a government of law) with ideas of responsiveness to the popular will (a government of majorities) and with loose ideas of social equality. By the presidency of Andrew Jackson, the word was too vague, too suggestive, and too valuable politically to retain any precise content or any real usefulness for political analysis.

In the natural-rights tradition, expressive freedoms and voting rights received little attention, and were by any analysis secondary to a vital and embracing concern for liberty and property. The most feared devil in that tradition, and also the focal issue in the quarrel with Britain, was the ever-present threat of servility and dependency. Americans proclaimed freedom as their goal, and freedom, above all else, meant economic independence or rights of property. If one takes seriously the rhetoric that preceded the revolution, the most important pledge to newly independent Americans was in this area. They could have protected access to nature and its resources, full individual control over the tools of production, and a private right to enjoy all the fruits of their honest labor except for those public expenditures that they approved through their own representative assemblies. Except for temporary interludes, white Americans would not have to be servants or wage laborers, taking orders from other men, denied the joys of purposeful planning and the intrinsic rewards of end-related work. Of course, eccentric individuals might choose economic servility, eschew ownership of a farm or shop, and seek good wages and economic security, but even this choice had to be free of any economic coercion, of the pressing stimulus of hunger or poverty. At the very least, the option of ownership and thus of realized freedom had to remain open in America.

It is ironic that property rights, in this natural or moral context, have not only fared worst of all in America, but have dropped from focal, political concern. Today only a small minority of Americans have property in the eighteenth-century sense of an exclusive claim to a part of nature joined with work, management, and consumption. Practically, most people do not have the remotest possibility of owning such property. Today we even use the word *property* for quite different objects, such as consumer goods, up to and including homes, and for investment wealth which does not involve either work or effective managerial rights. Most production now occurs in huge collectives with highly centralized management. In the modern corporation it is impossible to locate any property of the classic form, for aspects of it adhere to stockholders, with their speculative claims to a share of profits or to liquidation values, to those who actually manage the enterprise, to those who do the work, and finally to those who consume the goods or services. Today one could hardly think of a more radical proposal, or one more difficult to achieve, than a restoration of property rights to all Americans. In the Jeffersonian perspective, most of us would be classified as wage earners or mere employees. However well paid, however blessed with the tokens of respectability, we are still servile men and women, participants in a new and often very paternalistic and benevolent form of feudalism. Even the last bastions of property—farms and small retail outlets—seem threatened by corporate collectivism.

What happened? The story is much too complex for simple

answers. But it is important to note that the natural right to property was compromised from the very beginning. Because the overwhelming majority of the American farmers and mechanics who fought the Revolution or who formed new governments already owned and managed either land or the tools of their trade, the early concern over property was for the protection and conservation of already enjoyed rights, and not to insure equal access for the unpropertied or for later Americans. Even the most vociferous agrarians, soon fighting their battles against ascendant commercial and manufacturing interests, failed to remove the mote in their own eyes. They accepted their unearned social increments, which raised land prices in settled areas, or speculatively invested in unused and unneeded land, or countenanced absentee ownership, or, in the South, profited from slave labor. Wealth and special political privileges became, for so many of them, more compelling goals than a universally shared way of life.

Perhaps more important, it seems that a majority of Americans, and thus even of farmers, rejected the long-term option for America projected by a few consistent agrarians—a simple republic of virtuous yeomen or village artisans, harvesting the products of a fecund land and exchanging a surplus in Europe for needed manufactured goods, thus avoiding cities and factories and servile laborers and much of the apparatus of trade and high finance. Politically, emotionally, this vision had great appeal throughout the nineteenth century, and greatly influenced public policy. It still has some appeal. But so gradually as to be almost unnoticed, and not by any conscious series of decisions, it lost all support in reality.

By deed if not by creed, Americans fulfilled the vision of national greatness, of successful competition with European powers, that we often identify with Alexander Hamilton. By their adopted policies, they cast their decisive votes for rapid economic growth and a mixed economy, both of which encouraged, perhaps required, collective enterprise. They chose a course of development in no way consistent with a universal dispersion of the means of production. Even large-scale, efficient farming required wage laborers or slaves. The small shop and the independent artisan could not compete with factories filled with highly specialized, wage-dependent laborers. In this sense, Americans voted against a propertied society, eventually paying the price of almost universal economic servility for the glory of national greatness and the solace of abundance. But at least through the nineteenth century, the men who made the policy choices not only continued to celebrate older ideas of property but usually owned and managed real property. They escaped the servility, while those who suffered it most completely and often most willingly were aliens, imported laborers from Europe.

In a sense, the broadened franchise was a form of compensation for nonpropertied Americans. Even lowly wage employees could be citizens, and thus escape some of the stigma of their humble economic position. Had defenders of the old order been able to preserve the identity between property and franchise, then nonpropertied Americans might have fought even harder than they did for preemption and homestead rights, for restrictions on absentee ownership, for stiffer rules for incorporation, for greater managerial rights for wage laborers, or, in the path followed by Henry George, against the private exploitation of socially created scarcity by those who grabbed first. The widespread adoption of ballot voting (adopted in their earliest constitutions by North Carolina, Vermont, and New York) also allowed a new degree of political independence for farm and factory laborers, who could now more easily vote against the interests of employers. Later, when laborers turned to organization in order to win better working conditions and higher wages (they did not fight effectively for ownership and managerial rights), they found the vote an indispensable weapon.

Education eventually became as much of a nostrum as voting. By popular estimate, the right of free schooling is almost a modern natural right. Schools and vocational preparation eventually replaced ownership in our continued celebration of equal opportunity. Through time, the commitment to life, liberty, and property shifted to life (procedural guarantees), unhampered religious and verbal expression, the right to vote, and broad educational opportunities. If the old idea of property has any contemporary currency, it takes a strangely inverted form—the right to work, and not the right to own and manage the means of production. In a sense, we now proclaim the right of servility, for *work* usually denotes employment, a job, taking orders, and finding satisfaction in wages and not in the work experience. In a highly collectivized America, the image of a fulfilling life has shifted from the proximate ownership and artful management of property to a college education, high-status employment, investment success, and a high level of consumption.

We still have a balanced separation within our American governments, although ascendant federal power has eliminated much of the balancing effect of a division of power. Despite recent concern over the diminishing power of the federal Congress, or the enhanced power of the president, the federal bureaucracy, and the Supreme Court, there remains a balancing tension between the branches. The shifts in power and role are usually temporary. But despite the continuities, the now accepted two-party system very much altered the functioning of our governments, and more than anything else constitutes an unwritten addition to our constitutions.

The founding fathers knew and generally feared the type of factionalism that often characterized colonial politics. They hoped to avoid intense ideological divisions, which could wreck the new governments. Such hardheaded realists as Adams and Madison saw government in class terms, and expected unending clashes between gentlemen and simple men. But almost no one foresaw the type of broad-interest parties that later developed. The earliest party system, rooted both in conflict over the new constitution and in policy clashes in the Washington administration, actually came close to a divisive factionalism, for among the Federalists and the Republican leaders there were sharply different conceptions of America's future, quite divergent priorities in both economic and foreign policy, clear class and regional affinities, and at least a residue of ideological confrontation and passionate, noncompromising fervor. The Republicans won politically, but at the same time blended into their program a disarming bundle of Federalist policies, slowly defusing the explosive potentials of early party strife. The new parties, which were born out of the factional strife of the Jacksonian period and had less ideological glue, both reflected and helped develop a greater popular consensus on fundamental issues, merged more interests in loose coalitions, and assimilated the type of gamesmanship which made defeat bearable and effective opposition a form of patriotism. Each major party seemed to illustrate Madison's contention that, in a country so large, no one ideology or special-interest group could gain and retain dominance.

In a formal sense, political parties helped democratize American governments. The parties and announced candidates created a market for votes, and thus abetted more liberal franchise rules and massive efforts to get the people involved in campaigns and out to vote on election day. Out of the undirected clash of diverse local issues, the political party allowed a focusing as well as a simplification of issues, and thus greater likelihood of massed electoral power. The party system destroyed the indirect features of the federal Constitution, eliminating the deliberative role of the electoral college and assuring the election of announced senatorial candidates by the winning parties in state legislatures. In this sense, it abolished the last vestige of aristocracy and class mixture in government and reinforced at least the illusion of social equality.

Parties also posed a significant threat to the principle of separation. If one party gained a clear majority in every elective branch, a degree of party loyalty and discipline made possible close cooperation between Senate and House, or between Congress and the president. This cooperation, again, made the government more responsive to majorities and more of a threat to losing minorities. The party created a new type of president—an avowed candidate for office and head of the party. In order to win elections, parties had to seek candidates with broad, popular appeal, and also frame their platforms for the same purpose. The competition between two parties, the zeal of candidates, the promotional features of campaigns, all helped turn American politics into a form of popular entertainment, or into a fulfilling, participative sport. The allure of charismatic national candidates and the dominance of advertised national issues shifted some of the focus of political interest from local issues and candidates to the state and nation, and thus played a vital role in cementing forms of national loyalty and identity.

Formal changes can be deceitful. Political parties focused energy, but they did not necessarily widen choice. In the light of hotly contested, even if somewhat crude and vulgar, campaigns, of severely contested even if simplistic issues, it seemed that elites lost most of their function in nineteenth-century politics. The old prescription of mixed government—that aristocrats be isolated in a separate senate—no longer made any sense. Had John Adams lived on, he would have vainly protested that the only reason for the diminution of class conflict was the obvious fact that wealth and privilege had no completely won, and under the guise of popular democracy. But the explanation was surely not that simple. In a sense, the parties were themselves creatures of controlling oligarchs, and useful avenues of political leverage for the interested and the powerful who chose the issues and candidates for the great popular circus. Elections gave the large body of voters an intoxicating sense of political power, helped reinforce their loyalty to existing institutions, and muted any penchant for deep resentment or probing criticism. When dominated by national parties, national candidates, and carefully outfitted national issues, elections lost much of their originative role and became confirming referenda.

But these developments do not mean that political parties stripped the mass of people of effective political power. Their beliefs and prejudices were surely not so malleable that parties could manipulate them at will. Elections did present real even if narrowed choices. To an extent, any successful party had to conform to popular tastes. Even the party oligarchs had to don the dress and manners of the common man. What the party did do was shift operative political power to those able and willing to work within the party or to buy influence by financial contributions. Perhaps elections were in part the window dressing of American politics. But the two parties, at most times, were open to citizen participation, and even before party primaries often as receptive to eager workers or capable leaders as to wealthy contributors or massed special interests.

All these changes in our government must not obscure continuities. We are still institutionally very close to our eighteenth-century progenitors. Their "first principles" live on in our political habits, in the way we do things, and perhaps most of all in our almost reflexive political rhetoric. What often seems lacking is their vital concern with first principles, their continuous effort to blend lofty ideals with political realities. What recent president could bring to his speeches the historical knowledge, the legal sophistication, the familiarity with political theory that characterized Adams or Madison? What political leaders could now lecture to Americans with any depth on the subtleties of popular sovereignty, or the complex meanings in natural rights, or on the value of separation? Where, in our journals of opinion if not in our newspapers or in our campaigns, can one find the range of theoretical issues that marked even the most polemical literature before the American Revolution? Where in our present legislatures can we find the degree of political sophistication, as well as the civility, reflected by the quite ordinary delegates to the ratifying conventions of 1788?

These questions reveal my own concerns that, in spite of all our educational attainments and our brilliant mastery of technique, we may be closer to political illiteracy than our forebears. Perhaps, with the passing of time, a hazy political concensus or a slackening of vital political controversy destroyed the most conducive environment for wide-ranging political speculation. Except for a few isolated scholars, we have largely dropped an earlier and quite broadly based concern for the elusive and frustrating concerns of normative theory. Even the word *politics*, which once symbolized a branch of practical knowledge or a study of perennial moral issues in their public context, now symbolizes techniques of maintaining power or of manipulating people.

There are dangers in becoming political, in trying to extend our highest concerns beyond the most private and restricted arena. The burden of theoretical vindication often led our forefathers into hypocrisy. Later, when unchallenged by prophetic critics, the moral rectitude of Americans was a prelude to unforgivable arrogance. Also, the political task is now more difficult than in the past. Our Hellenistic Age confronts us with a confusing array of competing beliefs and preferences. It is difficult to launch a public inquiry on first principles in the absence of common philosophical traditions, a general agreement on goals, and a common language. But if I am at all correct in assuming that teleology—questions of ends and purposes—is today more critical in our public life than problems of means or techniques, then we must again deal with first principles. The working assumption behind this book is that we almost have to start with the best resource we have, with our own political heritage. It may be about the only thing we have in common.

Notes

1. Biography of an Idea

1. R. W. and A. J. Carlyle, *A History of Mediaeval Political Theory in the West*, 6 vols. (Edinburgh: William Blackwood & Sons, 1903–1936), I, 63–65.

2. Romans 13:1–4, King James Version.

3. Carlyle and Carlyle, I, 149–72, 210–50; II, 56–59; III, 96–102, 130–31, 140.

4. Ibid., VI, 44, 51–54, 241–49; Harold Laski, *The Foundations of Sovereignty and Other Essays* (New York: Harcourt, Brace and Company, 1921), pp. 211–12.

5. Carlyle and Carlyle, VI, 272–85; Duncan B. Forrester, "Martin Luther and John Calvin," in Leo Strauss and Joseph Cropsey, eds., *History of Political Philosophy* (Chicago: Rand McNally & Co., 1963), pp. 277–311.

6. John Calvin, *On God and Political Duty*, compiled and edited by John T. McNeil (New York: Liberal Arts Press, 1950), pp. 47–51, 74–77, 79–82.

7. George Buchanan, *The Art and Science of Government Among the Scots*, translated by Duncan H. MacNeill (n.p.: William MacClelan, 1964), pp. 21, 26–27, 28–41, 51, 58, 66–67, 72–73, 77, 88, 90–91, 96.

8. Théodore Bèze, *Du Droit des Magistrats*, introduction by Robert Kingdon (Geneva: Librarie Droz, 1970), pp. xxvi, xxxix, 3, 8–9, 13–14, 16–18, 44–53.

9. Harold Laski, ed., *A Defence of Liberty Against Tyranists*, a translation of *Vindiciae Contra Tyrannos* (London: G. Bell and Sons, 1924), pp. 34–36.

10. Ibid., p. 92.

11. Ibid., pp. 118–19.

12. Ibid., pp. 97–99, 104–11, 210, 226–29.

13. Jean Bodin, *The Six Books of a Commonwealth* [*République*], edited by Kenneth D. McRae, translated by Richard Knowles (Cambridge: Harvard University Press, 1962), pp. 60–68, 72–115, 184–85.

14. Johannes Althusius, *Politics*, translated by Frederick S. Carney (Boston: Beacon Press, 1964), pp. 4–6, 117–20.

15. Ibid., pp. 14, 68.

16. Ibid., pp. 93–98, 196–99.

17. John S. Marshall, *Hooker and the Anglican Tradition* (Sewanee, Tennessee: University of the South, 1963), pp. 102–108; Duncan B. Forrester, "Richard Hooker," in Strauss and Cropsey, *History of Political Philosophy*, pp. 314–22.

18. Walter Berns, "John Milton," in Strauss and Cropsey, *History of Political Philosophy*, pp. 397–412.

19. Robert Filmer, *Patriarcha*, a supplement to John Locke, *Two Treatises of Government*, Thomas Cook, ed. (New York: Hafner Publishing Co., 1947), pp. 251–308.

20. Thomas Hobbes, *Leviathan*, Michael Oakeshott, ed. (London: Collier-Macmillan, 1962), 134–42.

21. Algernon Sidney, *Discourses on Government*, 3 vols. (New York: Deare and Andrews, 1805), I, 320.

22. Ibid., I, 353.

23. Ibid., II, 61, 110, 362; III, 178, 248.

24. John Locke, *Two Treatises of Government*, Introduction and Notes by Peter Laslett (Cambridge: Cambridge University Press, 1960), pp. 301, 375–77.

25. Ibid., p. 414.

26. Enrich De Vattel, *The Law of Nations* (Philadelphia: T. and J. W. Johnson & Co., 1883), pp. 8–10.

27. Ibid., pp. 10–18.

2. *In Defense of Independence*

1. Edmund S. Morgan, ed., *Puritan Political Ideas, 1558–1794* (Indianapolis: Bobbs-Merrill, 1965), p. 175.

2. Alice Baldwin, *The New England Clergy and the American Revolution* (Durham: Duke University Press, 1928), p. 26.

3. Benjamin F. Wright, Jr., *American Interpretations of Natural Law* (Cambridge: Harvard University Press, 1931), pp. 24, 25–26.

4. Morgan, *Puritan Political Ideas*, p. 253.

5. Bernard Bailyn, ed., *Pamphlets of the American Revolution, 1750–1776*, vol. I (Cambridge: Harvard University Press, 1965), 237n.

6. Morgan, *Puritan Political Ideas*, p. 272.

7. Alden T. Vaughan, *Chronicles of the American Revolution*, originally compiled by Hezekiah Niles (New York: Grosset & Dunlap, 1965), p. 224.

8. Ben P. Poore, ed., *The Federal and State Constitutions, Colonial Charters, and Other Organic Laws of the United States*, 2 vols. (Washington: Government Printing Office, 1877), pp. 249–51.

9. Walter E. Volkomer, ed., *The Liberal Tradition in American Thought* (New York: G. P. Putman's Sons, 1969), pp. 39–40; George Haskins, *Law and Authority in Early Massachusetts* (New York: Macmillan and Co., 1960).

10. Michael G. Hall, Lawrence H. Leder, and Michael G. Kammen, eds., *The Glorious Revolution in America* (Chapel Hill: University of North Carolina Press, 1964), pp. 12–13, 20–22, 48–53.

11. Daniel Dulaney, "Considerations on the Propriety of Imposing Taxes in the British Colonies for the Purpose of Raising Revenue by Act of Parliament," in Merrill Jensen, ed., *Tracts of the American Revolution* (Indianapolis: Bobbs-Merrill, 1967), pp. 94–107.

12. Thomas Fitch, Jared Ingersoll, Ebenezer Silliman, and George Wyllys, "Reasons Why the British Colonies in America Should Not be Charged with Internal Taxes," in Bailyn, *Pamphlets*, I, 386–407.

13. John Dickinson, "Letters from a Farmer in Pennsylvania to the Inhabitants of the British Colonies," in Jensen, *Tracts*, pp. 127–63.

14. Richard Bland, "An Inquiry into the Rights of the British Colonies," in Jensen, *Tracts*, pp. 108–26.

15. William Hicks, "The Nature and Extent of Parliamentary Power," in Jensen, *Tracts*, pp. 164–84.

16. Stephen Hopkins, "An Essay on the Trade of the Northern Colonies," in Jensen, *Tracts*, pp. 3–18.

17. An early draft of "A Summary View of the Rights of British America," in Julian Boyd, ed., *The Papers of Thomas Jefferson*, 60 vols. (Princeton: Princeton University Press, 1950–), I, 121–37; the "Summary" is also available in Jensen, *Tracts*, pp. 256–76.

18. John Adams and Daniel Leonard, "Massachusettensis and Novanglus," in Jensen, *Tracts*, pp. 315–20, 328; George A. Peek, Jr., ed., *The Political Writings of John Adams: Representative Selections* (Indianapolis: Bobbs-Merrill, 1954), pp. 39, 43–48, 60–77.

19. Vaughan, *Chronicles*, pp. 42–53.

20. Ibid., pp. 54–62; Baldwin, *The New England Clergy*, pp. 117–18.

21. Charles H. McIlwain, *The American Revolution: A Constitutional Interpretation* (New York: Macmillan Co., 1923), pp. 1–17.

3. *Government of the People*

1. Gordon S. Wood, *The Creation of the American Republic, 1776–1787* (Chapel Hill: University of North Carolina Press, 1969), pp. 306–13.

2. Ben P. Poore, ed., *The Federal and State Constitutions, Colonial Charters, and Other Organic Laws of the United States* (Washington: Government Printing Office, 1877), pp. 1279–80.

3. Poore, *Federal and State Constitutions*, pp. 1613–28; Fletcher Green, *Constitutional Development in the South Atlantic States, 1776–1860* (New York: W. W. Norton, 1966), pp. 60–62; Elisha P. Douglass, *Rebels and Democrats: The Struggle for Equal Political Rights and Majority Rule During the American Revolution* (Chapel Hill: University of North Carolina Press, 1955), pp. 41–43.

4. Poore, *Federal and State Constitutions*, pp. 1908–12; Merrill D. Peterson, ed., *Democracy, Liberty, and Property: The State Constitutional Conventions of the 1820's* (Indianapolis: Bobbs-Merrill, 1966), pp. 271–85.

5. Wood, *Creation*, pp. 332–33; Poore, *Federal and State Constitutions*, pp. 273–78.

6. Wood, *Creation*, pp. 333–39; Douglass, *Rebels and Democrats*, pp. 248–78.

7. Poore, *Federal and State Constitutions*, pp. 1540–48.

8. Ibid., pp. 1857–87.

9. Douglass, *Rebels and Democrats*, pp. 49–50; Poore, *Federal and State Constitutions*, pp. 817–28.

10. Green, *Constitutional Development*, p. 59; Douglass, *Rebels and Democrats*, p. 126; Poore, *Federal and State Constitutions*, pp. 1409–14.

11. Poore, *Federal and State Constitutions*, pp. 1328–39.

12. Ibid., pp. 377–96.

13. Ibid., pp. 956–73; Douglass, *Rebels and Democrats*, pp. 144–74; *Journal of the Convention for Framing a Constitution of Government for the State of Massachusetts Bay* (Boston, 1832).

14. Jonathan Elliot, *The Debates in the Several State Conventions on the Adoption of the Federal Constitution etc.*, 5 vols. (Philadelphia: J. B. Lippincott Co., 1901), II, 434, 456–58; James Madison, *Notes on Debates in the Federal Convention of 1787*, introduction by Adrienne Koch (New York: W. W. Norton, 1969), pp. 90, 129–30.

15. Madison, *Notes*, pp. 229, 213, 491, 243.

16. Ibid., pp. 350–52.

17. Ibid., pp. 348, 352–53.

18. Ibid., p. 649.

19. Ibid., p. 341.

20. *The Federalist Papers*, introduced by Clinton Rossiter (New York: New American Library—Mentor, 1961), pp. 466–68; Elliot, *Debates*, II, 489–90.

21. *Federalist Papers*, p. 470.

4. *The Legal and Moral Heritage*

1. James E. Holton, "Marcus Tullius Cicero," in Leo Strauss and Joseph Cropsey, eds., *History of Political Philosophy* (Chicago: Rand McNally & Co., 1963), p. 144.

2. Romans 2: 14–15, *New English Bible* (Cambridge: Cambridge University Press, 1970).

3. R. W. and A. J. Carlyle, *A History of Mediaeval Political Theory in the West*, 6 vols. (Edinburgh: William Blackwood & Sons, 1903–1936), II, 1–56, 102–41.

4. Duncan B. Forrester, "Martin Luther and John Calvin," in Strauss and Cropsey, *History of Political Philosophy*, pp. 277–313; John Calvin, *On God and Political Duty*, compiled and edited by John T. McNeil (New York: Liberal Arts Press, 1950), pp. 65–68.

5. Harold Laski, ed., *A Defence of Liberty Against Tyranists*, a translation of *Vindiciae Contra Tyrannos* (London: G. Bell and Sons, 1924), pp. 139–53.

6. Ibid., p. 190.

7. Carlyle and Carlyle, I, 132–40; V, 16–20.

8. Laski, *Vindiciae*, pp. 140, 163.

9. Johannes Althusius, *Politics*, translated by Frederick S. Carney (Boston: Beacon Press, 1964), p. 90; John Locke, *Two Treatises of Government*, Introduction and Notes by Peter Laslett (Cambridge: Cambridge University Press, 1960), p. 346.

10. Althusius, *Politics*, pp. 12–13, 19, 92, 116.

11. Thomas Hobbes, *Leviathan: or the Matter, Forms and Powers of a Commonwealth Ecclesiastical and Civil* (London: Collier Books, 1962), passim.

12. Algernon Sidney, *Discourses on Government*, 3 vols. (New York: Deare and Andrews, 1805), III, 36, 68–69.

13. Ibid., p. 185.

14. Locke, *Two Treatises* (Laslett edition), pp. 176–77, 348.

15. Ibid., pp. 327–44.

16. Enrich de Vattel, *The Law of Nations* (Philadelphia: T. and J. W. Johnson & Co., 1883), pp. viii–ix, 37, 44, 56.

17. Samuel Pufendorf, *De Jure Naturae et Gentium Libri Octo*, translated by C. H. and W. A. Oldfather, 2 vols., in *The Classics of International Law*, James Brown Scott, ed. (Oxford: Clarendon Press, 1934), II, 508, 25–27, 536.

18. Jean Jacques Burlamaqui, *The Principles of Natural Law*, translated by Nugent (London: J. Nourse, 1748), pp. 46, 51, 77–78, 89–97.

19. Bernard Bailyn, *The Ideological Origins of the American Revolution* (Cambridge: Harvard University Press, 1967).

5. In a Revolutionary Context

1. Edmund S. Morgan, ed., *Puritan Political Ideas*, 1558–1794 (Indianapolis: Bobbs–Merrill, 1965), pp. 335–37.

2. Ibid., p. 338.

3. Merrill Jensen, ed., *Tracts of the American Revolution* (Indianapolis: Bobbs-Merrill, 1967), p. 83; Alice Baldwin, *The New England Clergy and the American Revolution* (Durham: Duke University Press, 1928), pp. 101–102.

4. Alden T. Vaughan, *Chronicles of the American Revolution* (New York: Grosset & Dunlap, 1965), pp. 10–15; Edmund S. and Helen M. Morgan, *The Stamp Act Crisis* (Chapel Hill: University of North Carolina Press, 1953), pp. 103–106; James Otis, "The Rights of the British Colonies Asserted and Proved," in Jensen, *Tracts*, p. 24; John Adams, "A Dissertation on the Canon and Feudal Law," in George A. Peek, Jr., ed., *The Political Writings of John Adams: Representative Selections* (Indianapolis: Bobbs-Merrill, (1954), pp. 19–20.

5. Samuel Adams, "A State of the Rights of the Colonists," in Jensen, *Tracts*, pp. 235–38; Vaughan, *Chronicles of the American Revolution*, p. 64; Morgan and Morgan, *The Stamp Act Crisis*, p. 102.

6. Julian Boyd, ed., *The Papers of Thomas Jefferson*, 60 vols. (Princeton: Princeton University Press, 1950–), I, 121–37.

7. Vaughan, *Chronicles of the American Revolution*, p. 76.

6. Rights in the American Republic

1. *The Works of John Adams*, Charles Francis Adams, ed., 10 vols. (Boston, 1850–1856), VI, 56.

2. This and all subsequent references to state constitutions derive from Ben P. Poore, ed., *The Federal and State Constitutions, Colonial Charters, and Other Organic Laws of the United States* (Washington: Government Printing Office, 1877).

3. *Journal of the Convention for Framing a Constitution for the State of Massachusetts Bay* (Boston, 1832), pp. 37–46.

4. Leonard W. Levy, ed., *Freedom of the Press from Zenger to Jefferson* (Indianapolis: Bobbs-Merrill, 1966), pp. xix–lv.

5. James Madison, *Notes on Debates in the Federal Convention of 1787*, introduction by Adrienne Koch (New York: W. W. Norton, 1969), pp. 627–40.

6. *The Federalist Papers* (New York: New American Library—Mentor, 1961), pp. 510–15.

7. James M. Smith, *Freedom's Fetters: The Alien and Sedition Laws and American Civil Liberties* (Ithaca: Cornell University Press, 1956), passim; Jonathan Elliott, *The Debates in the Several State Conventions on the Adoption of the Federal Constitution etc.*, 5 vols. (Philadelphia: J. B. Lippincott Co., 1901), IV, 569–77.

8. Levy, *Freedom of the Press*, pp. lxx–lxxvii.

7. *Mixture and Separation: The Complex Legacy*

1. M. J. C. Vile, *Constitutionalism and the Separation of Powers* (Oxford: Clarenden Press, 1967), pp. 135–38.

2. W. B. Gwyn, *The Meaning of the Separation of Powers*, in Tulane Studies in Political Science, IX (New Orleans: Tulane University Press, (1965), pp. 24–25; Algernon Sidney, *Discourses on Government*, 3 vols. New York: Deare and Andrews, 1805), II, 138.

3. James Harrington, *The Commonwealth of Oceana* (London: George Rutledge and Sons, 1887), passim; J. R. Pole, *Political Representation in England and the Origins of the American Republic* (New York: St. Martin's Press, 1966), pp. 8–12.

4. Thomas Paine, *Common Sense and Other Political Writings*, ed. by Nelson F. Adkins (New York: Liberal Arts Press, 1953), pp. 4–18; Julian Boyd, ed., *The Papers of Thomas Jefferson*, 60 vols. (Princeton: Princeton University Press, 1950–), I, 337–47, 348–55, 503–506; Jefferson, *Notes on Virginia*, ed. by William Peden (Chapel Hill: University of North Carolina Press, 1955), pp. 118–29.

5. John Adams, *A Defence of the Constitutions of Government of the United States of America Against the Attack of M. Turgot etc.* (Boston: Budd and Bartram, 1797), 3 volumes, passim, and III, 506.

6. Vile, pp. 35–44, passim.

7. Gwyn, pp. 39–52.

8. Ibid., pp. 69–80; John Locke, *Two Treatises of Government* (Laslett edition) (Cambridge: Cambridge University Press, 1960), pp. 412–19.

9. Gwyn, pp. 82–90.

10. Baron de Montesquieu, *The Spirit of the Laws*, translated by Thomas Nugent (New York: Hafner Publishing Company, 1966), pp. 150–62, passim.

8. *Balanced Separation: The American Choice*

1. This and the following analyses of state constitutions rely on the constitutions as printed in Ben P. Poore, ed., *The Federal and State Constitutions, Colonial Charters, and Other Organic Laws of the United States* (Washington, Government Printing Office, 1877).

2. This and subsequent references to John Adams' views on mixed government reflect an analysis of his *A Defence of the Constitutions of Government of the United States of America Against the Attack of M. Turgot etc.*, 3 vols. (Boston: Budd and Bartram, 1797).

3. Gordon S. Wood, *The Creation of the American Republic, 1776–1787* (Chapel Hill: University of North Carolina Press, 1969), pp. 233–37; Elisha P. Douglass, *Rebels and Democrats: The Struggle for Equal Political Rights and Majority Rule During the American Revolution* (Chapel Hill: University of North Carolina Press, 1955), pp. 276–77.

4. "Report of the Council of Censors, 1783," in *The Proceedings relative to Calling the Conventions of 1776 and 1790. The Minutes of the Convention etc.* (Harrisburg, 1825), pp. 66–128.

5. Ibid., pp. 79–85, 116–17.

6. *Proceedings of the Conventions of the Province of Maryland held at the City of Annapolis in 1774, 1775, and 1776* (Baltimore: James Lucas & E. K. Deaver, 1836), p. 302; *Journal of the Convention for Framing a Constitution of Government for the State of Massachusetts Bay* (Boston, 1832), pp. 95, 197.

7. James Madison, *Notes on Debates in the Federal Convention of 1787* (New York: W. W. Norton, 1969), pp. 233–35, 322–25.

8. Ibid., pp. 82–83, 110, 129, 126, 114, 182.

9. *The Federalist Papers* (New York: New American Library— Mentor, 1961), pp. 376–407.

10. Madison, *Notes*, p. 451.

11. Ibid., pp. 304–305.

12. Ibid., pp. 61, 311–12, 326–27, 338, 341–42.

13. *Federalist Papers*, pp. 300–324.

14. Jonathan Elliot, *The Debates in the Several State Conventions on the Adoption of the Federal Constitution etc.*, 5 vols. (Philadelphia: J. B. Lippincott Co., 1901), IV, 328–29; II, 286–325; III, 164–65.

15. Ibid., II, 479; IV, 73–75; II, 242–51.

Index